Uncle John's
BATHROOM READER®
PLUNGES INTO
MICHIGAN

Uncle John's BATHROOM READER® PLUNGES INTO MICHIGAN

Bathroom Readers' Hysterical Society
San Diego, California

Uncle John's Bathroom Reader
Plunges into Michigan

For information, write The Bathroom Readers' Hysterical Society
Portable Press, 5880 Oberlin Drive, San Diego, CA 92121
e-mail: unclejohn@advmkt.com

ISBN 13: 978-1-59223-267-3
ISBN 10: 1-59223-267-1

Library of Congress Cataloging-in-Publication Data
is available

Printed in the United States of America
First printing: October 2005

05 06 07 08 09   10 9 8 7 6 5 4 3 2 1

Project Team

Allen Orso, Publisher

JoAnn Padgett, Director, Editorial and Production

Jennifer Browning, Production Editor

Vincent Archuletta, Cover Design

Heather McElwain, Copyeditor

Tamar Schwartz, Proofreader

The Bathroom Readers' Hysterical Society sincerely thanks the following additional people whose advice and assistance made this book possible.

Barb Barden

Beth Fhaner

Cynthia Francisco

Mary Lou GoForth

Kristine Hemp

Gordon Javna

Charlotte Kearns

Julia Papps

Brian Regan

Michelle Sedgwick

Sydney Stanley

Olivia Tabert

Deborah Taylor

Jennifer Thornton

Connie Vazquez

Hysterical Scholars

The Bathroom Readers' Hysterical Society sincerely thanks the following talented people who contributed selections to this work.

Jennifer Anderson
Annie Bauers
Jennifer Browning
Michael Cade
Myles Callum
Jennifer Carlisle
Ally Chumley
Deborah Dimminger
Karen Dybis
Laurie Enyon
Mali Feld
Kathryn Grogman
Chris Gullen
Cole Haddon
Brian Hudson
Cate Huguelet
Andy Levy-Ajzenkopf
Maximilian Longley
Michael Loomis
Jane Lott

Felisa Madrigal
Lea Markson
Kirsten Miller
Jonathan Moeller
Arthur Montague
Ryan Murphy
Colleen O'Neill
Darrin Pack
Ken Padgett
MJ Plaster
John Scalzi
Mali Schantz-Feld
Terri Schlichenmeyer
Leo Siren
Betty Sleep
Susan Steiner
Olivia Tabert
Stephanie Villanova
Lorie Witkop
Julia Wittner

Contents

Along the Road

I Saw It in Michigan 3

Off the Beaten Track 79

Making the Best of a Cold Situation 99

Museum Mania 118

Let the Good Times Roll! 207

Around the State

Dam Nation 7

What's So Great About the Great Lakes? 13

Digging the Dunes 29

From Hell to Zilwaukee 142

Lasting Impressions 184

A Wet Mitten 201

Autopia

Birth of a Giant, Part I 9

The Best Business Deal in U.S. History, Part I 75

Birth of a Giant, Part II 107

Curious Cars 126

Birth of a Giant, Part III 177

The Best Business Deal in U.S. History, Part II 187

Wheels 198
The Best Business Deal In U.S. History, Part III 222
The World's First Muscle Car .288

Business in Michigan

Bohemian Rhapsody 22
Through the Mill 85
Pop Goes Detroit 111
Upjohn's Pills 164
The Birth of Gerber 180
Shafted in Detroit 185
Top Pop 243
Making a Big Noise 275
The Ten Cents Store 285

Get Smart! School Spirit

Go Spartans! 64
Go Wolverines! 65
We Got Game 81
Superstitions 101 124

History

House of David 17
Four Flags 61
Detroit's Whiskey River 66
"Strang" but True 72
The Resort That Segregation Built 97
Let Them Eat Pancakes! 130
Battle of the Brans 147

The Big Mac 211
Yo Ho Ho and a Barrel of Venison 225
Michigan's Lumber Industry .237
No Kiddie Without a Christmas 241
Spilling His Guts 269
B-24s: Built for the Road Ahead 271
The Cherry Capital of the World 278
Walk the Plank? No, Drive It 295

Hometowns

A Touch of Dutch 32
Capital City, Lansing 70
Middle of the Mitten 102
Michigan's "Little Bavaria" 115
A Little Town on the Way Up 136
Furniture Central 151
B&B Country 193
Land of Sunsets and Stones .231
Gateway to the U.P. 245
Anatomy of a Village 264
River View 283

It's Official

Odd Michigan Laws 113
State of Confusion 190
Official Business 195
Musical Mystery Tour 209
A Banner Unfurled 233

Lights! Camera! Action!

Motor City Movies 15

I Want My M(ichigan) TV! 39

For Love of the Game 90

Literary Michigan

Hemingway Country 132

A Miller's Tale 174

Tales of the Third Coast 250

Michigan's a Good Sport

Baseball in Beards 20

End of an Era 37

Bowled Over 42

Hoop Magic 45

A Bowler's Paradise 94

Third Time's the Charm 203

Howe Amazing! 205

Octopi on Ice 215

It's Beautiful to Be Belgian 254

UM vs. OSU 256

Pass the Turkey 261

Pistons by the Numbers 293

Mixed Bag

Pick a Pocket 54

Shipwreck! 104

Paczki Fever 145

Smelt Dipping 101 168

The Grand Dame 235

A Fun Run 248

We Get Letters 259

Treasures from the Deep 298

Native Sons and Daughters

Godfather of the U.P. 92

"I Am a Ford, Not a Lincoln" 120

Boy Wonder 153

Surfmen, USA 160

Magichigans 162

Battle Creek's Gr-r-reatest Son 172

Which Michigander Am I? 228

Puzzles

Celebrity Michigan 52

A Model Puzzle 88

Road Shows 166

Bragging Rights 182

Take a Michi-gander at This 220

Sing a Song of Michigan

Michigan in Song 26

Michigan Rocks! 57

Motown's Greatest? 138

Berry Gordy Jr. 217

Talking the Talk

Yoopers and Lopers and Trolls, Oh My! 4

Do You Speak Michigan? 157

Yippee for Yoopers! 170

Tall Tales

Joe Bunyan 1

Ghostly Girls 34

A Spooky De-Light 49

"One Day, Eino and Toivo ..." .266

Answers 300

Preface

With two peninsulas and miles of shoreline, our intrepid contributors had a lot of ground—and coast—to cover. When all was said and done, we could have filled this book with twice the number of tales. Michigan is a fascinating state with a rich history and lots of colorful people and places. We had a hard time narrowing down our selections. Here is a sample of some of the stories we could not resist telling.

History: Michigan's history is filled with pirates, whiskey smuggling, lumberjacks, and even a "Boy Governor." Industrious Michiganders have had a hand in everything from creating the world's largest cherry pie to producing record numbers of B-24 bombers for World War II. One native even created a new branch of science.

Hometowns: With so many great places to live or visit it sure would be hard to decide if you wanted to be a Yooper or Troll. We covered some of Michigan's most memorable cities. In the process, we came up with a Michigander test. Try to answer the questions in "Do You Speak Michigan?" on page 157. You may be surprised at what you don't know.

Local Fare: For lunch a Michigander might enjoy a pasty washed down with a Vernor's ginger ale. If that does not fill you up, a paczki and Faygo makes a great afternoon snack. If you are a fan of any of these delectable taste treats, you will enjoy learning about their historic origins.

Michigan Means Business: The birth of the automotive industry is a fascinating saga and we hope you learn something that you did not already know. Besides giving birth to the automobile, Michigan also has given us such treasured American icons as Jiffy corn muffins, Kresge and Kmart, Motown, and Battle Creek's gr-r-reat cereals!

Michigan Is a Great Sport: Michiganders love the great outdoors and participate in all kinds of activities from hunting and skiing to water sports of all kinds. Indoor sports like ten pins or the unique game of feather bowling are popular too, as are armchair ones. Few states field as many championship teams as Michigan. There is no shortage of teams to support, whether you root for the Spartans or Wolverines or the Lions, Pistons, Redwings, or Tigers. We hope you enjoy our take on your favorite team.

With all these treasures, no wonder the state motto is, "If you seek a pleasant peninsula, look about you."

Bathroom Readers' Hysterical Society

Joe Bunyan

Building mountains, straightening crooked rivers, leveling forests—though his exploits are obviously fanciful, Paul Bunyan may be based on an actual person, logging boss Fabian Fournier.

Born in Quebec, Canada, around 1845, Fabian "Joe" Fournier immigrated to the Saginaw Bay area in the 1860s. With over 17 million acres of virgin pine forest, Michigan was the epicenter of a booming timber industry. It took a tough man to withstand the long hours, low pay (around $1 per day), grueling labor, and isolation of tree felling. Adept with an ax and a natural leader, Fournier soon hacked his way to the head of the camp. Joe ran a tight camp with zero tolerance for laziness, but when camp broke for the season he made tracks for Bay City, bound for some rowdy good times.

Joe was a fearsome brawler. He stood six feet tall and was said to possess the strength of three men. In addition, he made frequent use of another unusual attribute—a double row of teeth. Loggers who witnessed Joe's feats told tales of him biting chunks of wood from the bar and leaping through the air to dig his hobnail boots into the walls. Before Joe and his crew had finished flattening the Saginaw forests, Joe's legend was already larger than life. But like Michigan's lofty pines, even the mightiest man can fall. In late 1875 Fournier suffered a deadly blow at the hands of a rival lumbering tough.

Paul Bunyan Grows . . . and Grows

When news of Joe's murder hit the papers, loggers spent nights spinning his story and his deeds magnified with each retelling. On August 10, 1906, the *Oscoda/AuSable Press* ran a fantastical story about a lumberjack named Paul Bunyan called "Round River," by James MacGillivray. The story is the earliest known version of a Paul Bunyan tale, and some elements—a fellow with two sets of teeth, for one—echoed traits of Joe Fournier.

In 1914 the Red River Lumber Company adopted Bunyan as the company mascot. Artist W. B. Laughead's illustration captured the public's imagination and became the prototype for Bunyan as we know him: a burly, mustached giant clad in boots and flannel. Before long Paul's story had been retold in children's books, paintings, and even an opera. Stories of Fournier's unruly ways faded into the background as Paul's virtues and heroic feats came to symbolize the grit of a nation.

As Joe's feats had been exaggerated, so too were Paul Bunyan's adventures. A 1958 Disney cartoon claimed he stood over ten ax handles high. After razing the Michigan woods, Paul and a colossal blue ox, Babe, journeyed westward, blazing a trail straight to the Pacific and creating major American landforms in the process. As his popularity increased, many states vied for ownership of Paul until his alleged birthplace ranged from Maine to California. Though everyone wants a piece of Paul Bunyan, he owes his beginnings to Michigan, the fireside tales of bygone lumber camps, and crazy ol' Saginaw Joe.

I Saw It in Michigan

*Some seemingly normal objects are put to peculiar uses
in Michigan. Here are a few of Uncle John's favorites.*

"Snow Thermometer": This Michigan icon is a 32-foot-high
gauge to measure local snowfall.
Where: U.S. 41, in the Keweenaw Peninsula, north of Calumet.

Deer whistles: These whistles generate sounds as wind travels
through them and are supposed to warn deer, elk, and the like
of approaching vehicles.
Where: Bolted on fronts of cars, trucks, and motorcycles.

Singing sands: These sand particles make a resonating sound
when you walk upon them.
Where: Along the coast of Lake Michigan and in Bete Gris.

Bottle House: Made out of more than 60,000 soft drink
bottles, it was built in 1941 by John J. Makinen, the owner of
the Northwestern Bottling Works—a local bottling factory. The
bottles were laid on their sides and the bottoms of the bottles
form the outside walls. It is a National Historic Registered site
and is the location of the Kaleva Historical Museum.
Where: Kaleva, Michigan.

Yoopers and Lopers and Trolls, Oh My!

Here's a handy guide to speaking like a Michigander.

Big Mac: The Mackinac Bridge, which connects the upper and lower peninsulas. *See Mac*

The Bridge: In Detroit, the Ambassador Bridge; in Port Huron, the Blue Water Bridge; in the rest of Michigan, the Mackinac Bridge.

Choppers: Fur-lined leather mittens, in the U.P.

Down South: Ohio.

Fudgies: Mackinac Island tourists, so called because they buy and eat a lot of Mackinac Island fudge.

Glove Box: Commonly referred to as a glove compartment elsewhere.

Green and White: Michigan State University, or their football team; a reference to the school colors. Despite what you may have heard, the best football team in Michigan. *See Maize and Blue*

Hockeytown: Detroit nickname because of the multiple-cup-winning Detroit Red Wings.

Loper: A resident of the Lower Peninsula. *See Troll and Yooper*

Mac: The Mackinac Bridge, which connects the upper and lower peninsulas. *See Big Mac*

Maize and Blue: The University of Michigan, or their football team; a reference to the school colors. Despite what you may have heard, the best football team in Michigan. *See Green and White*

Michigan Bush: Squat, orange-and-white-striped plastic "hedgerows" that grow wild on Michigan highways between March and November. Natural habitat of the Michigan Orange-Vested Construction Worker.

Michigan Left: A legal left-hand turn made on a divided highway, executed by passing the street you want, U-turning across the median, and then making a right-hand turn onto the desired street.

Mitten: The Lower Peninsula, because it looks like one.

Pop: Proper name for carbonated beverages.

Soo: Sault Ste. Marie ("Sault" is pronounced "Soo," honestly), the oldest city in Michigan. Also used to refer to its sister city, Sault Ste. Marie, Ontario, Canada, on the other side of the St. Marys River.

Swampers: Yooper name for rubber boots or rubber hip-waders.

Thumb: The Lower Peninsula's own peninsula, jutting out into Lake Huron. *See Mitten*

Toll Collector: A resident of Mackinac City or St. Ignace, the cities on either end of the Big Mac.

Troll: Someone from the Lower Peninsula, so called because they live "under the Bridge." *See Loper and Trooper*

Trooper: A Troll who moves to Yooperland.

Tuque: A knit winter hat, in the U.P.

Union: Instead of a generic term, a specific reference to the United Automobile, Aerospace and Agricultural Implement Workers of America, or UAW.

Up North: For anyone living south of Flint, a summer vacation destination. For everyone living north of Flint, home.

Yooper: A resident of the Upper Peninsula, derived from the initials "U.P." Hence, Yooperland for the Upper Peninsula.

MARVELOUS MOOSE

Newberry, Michigan, claims the title "Official Moose Capital of Michigan." Here are some facts to impress your friends.

400–600: Estimated moose population in the western U.P.

60 inches: Average span of moose antlers. Why do moose have such big antlers? For better radio reception.

1,200 pounds: Average weight of a bull moose.

50: Percentage of body weight moose gain for winter months and lose in the spring.

25–30: Average number of calves a moose cow births in her lifetime.

Dam Nation

The State of Michigan vs. the beavers. Who will prevail?

One of the most intriguing environmental legal battles took place from 1997 to 1998 between the Spring Pond beavers of Marne, Michigan, and the Michigan Department of Environmental Quality (DEQ). The beavers, doing what beavers do best, dared to construct a dam on Stephen Tvedten's property.

Charge: Illegal Dam Building

The trouble began when Ryan DeVries, one of Tvedten's neighbors, complained to the Michigan DEQ about flooding on his property caused by a dam located on Tvedten's property. The DEQ responded to DeVries instead of Tvedten, accusing DeVries of participating in unauthorized activity, specifically the construction of two illegal wood debris dams across an outlet stream of Spring Pond. Such illegal activities carried a fine of $10,000 per day. The DEQ ordered DeVries to cease and desist construction on the dams and to remove all wood and brush in time for a site inspection by DEQ agents.

The Rebuttal

DeVries forwarded the letter from the DEQ to Tvedten, because it was Tvedten's dam, not his. When Tvedten received the DEQ letter from DeVries, he responded to the DEQ on the Spring Pond beavers' behalf. Tvedten asked all the right questions:

- Was the DEQ discriminating against the Spring Pond beavers, or were all beavers required to file a permit before beginning dam construction?

- To prove that there had been no discrimination, Tvedten asked for copies of dam permits filed by other beavers.

- He informed the DEQ that if they were serious about dam removal, they had better tell the proper parties—the beavers.

- Mr. Tvedten was especially concerned that the state preserve the beavers' civil rights. Was the state going to arrest the beavers? Would the beavers be read their rights? Because they were indigent, would the state provide legal representation?

He concluded, "In my humble opinion, the Spring Pond beavers have a right to build their . . . unauthorized dams as long as the sky is blue, the grass is green, and water flows downstream." The Michigan DEQ inspected the site and dropped the investigation after the dam was removed and the beavers moved on.

Epilogue

It is rumored that the beavers have returned to Spring Pond, the original scene of the crime, for an encore performance. The saga continues.

Birth of a Giant, Part I

Ever wonder why Uncle John drives an old Buick? Part of the reason
is because he likes old Buicks . . . and part is because David Buick
was more than a car manufacturer—he was a bathroom hero.
From Absolutely Absorbing, *here's the story of Mr. Buick . . .*
and the giant auto company that grew out of his work.

A Bathroom Hero

In 1882 the Alex Manufacturing Company of Detroit, a maker
of iron toilet bowls and wooden water-closet tanks, went bank-
rupt. The company's plant foreman, David Dunbar Buick, and a
partner, William Sherwood, took over the company, renamed it
Buick and Sherwood, and nursed it back to health.

Buick was an ingenious man; he received 13 patents on
various plumbing fixtures between 1881 and 1889, including
valves, flushing devices, and even a lawn sprinkler. But his
most significant patent was for an improved method of fixing
white porcelain onto an iron surface, such as a bathtub. In
other words, Buick is the father of the modern bathtub.

Quit When You're a Head

If there was ever a time to be in the plumbing business, the
early 1890s was it. "With the rapid growth of urban areas and
the great increase in the adoption of indoor plumbing facilities,

David Buick's fortune would seem to have been assured," George S. May writes in *A Most Unique Machine*. "Instead, he threw this away in favor of another interest—gasoline engines and automobiles."

In 1899 Buick and Sherwood sold their company for $100,000. Buick used his share of the money to found the Buick Auto-Vim and Power Company, which manufactured gasoline motors for use in industry, in farming, and on riverboats. In 1902 Buick changed the name to the Buick Manufacturing Company and began making automobiles. Buick's automobile engine was one of the most advanced of its day, but Buick himself was apparently a terrible businessman.

Down the Drain

By the fall of 1903 Buick had used up all the money he'd made selling his plumbing business . . . and still owed so much money to Briscoe Brothers (his sheet metal supplier) that he signed over ownership of nearly the entire company to Benjamin and Frank Briscoe—on the condition that he'd get it back when he repaid them. But Buick never did repay them, so in September 1903 the Briscoes sold their stake in the company to Flint Wagon Works, a carriage maker in Flint, Michigan.

Buick, still in debt, stayed on to manage the company for the new owners.

Enter William Durant

The owners of the Flint Wagon Works quickly came to realize that running an automobile company was going to cost a lot more than they were willing to spend. Furthermore, for all his talent as an inventor, David Buick was a terrible manager; the auto company would probably never make any money as long as he was in charge. So in 1904 Flint Wagon Works shoved David Buick aside and turned the reins of the company over to William "Billy" Crapo Durant, owner of a competing carriage company in Flint. Their plan: Flint Wagon Works would continue to own a stake in Buick, but Durant would run it and would raise new money by selling stock to outside investors. If anyone could turn Buick around, Billy Durant could. In 1884 Durant, then a young insurance salesman, had seen a horse-drawn road cart while on a selling trip in Michigan. He was so impressed with the design that he abandoned insurance, bought the patent rights to the cart, and, together with a hardware clerk named Josiah Dallas Dort, formed a company to manufacture and sell the cart.

Tycoon

By the time Durant joined Buick in November 1904, he'd built Durant-Dort into the largest carriage company in the nation, with 14 factories across the United States and Canada and a nationwide network of dealerships that sold more than 75,000 carriages a year. It was an awesome achievement, and the owners of the Flint Wagon Works hoped that Durant would be able to work the same magic at Buick.

Boo-ick

As for David Buick: He retained the title of company secretary and still had a seat on the board of directors, but his days of running the firm that bore his name were over. In fact, the Flint

Wagon Works considered changing the name to the Durant Motor Company to capitalize on Durant's business fame. Durant, however, insisted that the car retain the name of its inventor, even though he was worried that the public might mispronounce it "Boo-ick."

For Part II, turn to page 107.

THE NOVA THAT "DOESN'T GO"

According to popular legend, the Chevy Nova had dismal sales in Latin American countries because the word sounds like "no va," which translates to "doesn't go."

The legend began circulating in business manuals and seminars in the 1980s warning of the follies of failing to do adequate market research before releasing products in foreign markets. It spread from there to newspaper columnists.

The Truth: When Chevrolet first released the Nova in Mexico, Venezuela, and other Spanish-speaking countries in 1972, the car sold just fine—even better than expected in Venezuela. According to www.snopes.com, the very nature of the tale is absurd: "Assuming that Spanish speakers would naturally see the word 'nova' as equivalent to the phrase 'no va' and think, 'Hey, this car doesn't go!' is akin to assuming that English speakers would spurn a dinette set sold under the name *Notable* because nobody wants a dinette set that doesn't include a table."

What's So Great About the Great Lakes?

Everyone knows the mnemonic device, HOMES, used to remember the names of all five Great Lakes, but what else do you know about the largest fresh surface water system on earth? For answers, turn to page 300.

1. What lake does not have a shoreline in Michigan?

2. What lake does not share a border with Canada?

3. In his ballad of the sinking of the great iron ore ship, the *Edmund Fitzgerald*, what is the lake that Gordon Lightfoot sings about?

4. Of the five, which lake is the shallowest and warmest? Hint: it is reputed to have the best walleye fishery in the world.

5. What is the most populous U.S. city on the shores of the Great Lakes? And on which lake?

6. Isle Royale, the only U.S. National Park on the Great Lakes, is located on which lake?

7. The SS *Badger* is a ferry that allows travelers and their vehicles to get from Ludington, Michigan, to Manitowoc, Wisconsin, thereby taking a shortcut across what lake?

8. Freighters that pass through the Soo Locks at Sault Ste. Marie undergo a 21-foot drop from one lake to the next. Which Great Lake's water level is 21 feet higher than its nearest neighbor at the Soo Locks?

9. The Mackinac Bridge, suspended over the Straits of Mackinac, connects which two Great Lakes?

10. The "mitten" shape of the state of Michigan is formed by the boundaries of which three Great Lakes?

DID YOU KNOW?

The Great Lakes have long been said to host large serpentine beasts, similar to Scotland's famous Loch Ness Monster. Lake Superior has "Pressie"—named after the Presque Isle River—and Lake Erie has "South Bay Bessie."

Pressie appears to be the most elusive, perhaps owing to the size of Lake Superior, but also is the more ancient of the two. Sightings date back to the Ojibway native people as well as several boat crews in the late 1890s but continue to the present day. Pressie is described as 75 feet long with a long neck and whalelike tail.

John Schaffner, editor of the *Ottawa County Beacon,* has gathered data on close to a dozen reported sightings of Bessie, the earliest dating to 1960. Most people who claim to have seen Bessie describe a 30- to 50-foot-long serpent with humps. A group of businessmen once offered a $150,000 reward for her live capture.

Motor City Movies

Some films from and around Detroit.

RoboCop (1987)

There's a new cop in Detroit, and this one is made of metal. He's bulletproof and not too gentle when arresting the bad guys—maybe a good thing, because the Detroit in this film is so violent it makes the Wild West look like a tea party. This science-fiction film introduced American audiences to Dutch director Paul Verhoeven's special blend of blood-soaked violence and black humor.

The Crow (1994)

The dark, drizzly city of the film is never named, but we know it is Detroit because of the "Devil's Night" tradition and the fact that James O'Barr, the creator of the comic book on which the film is based, is from Detroit. The story features a murdered rock guitarist who returns from the dead to avenge his death and the death of his fiancée.

Grosse Pointe Blank (1997)

While people are often ambivalent about high school reunions, Martin Blank (John Cusack) has more reasons than most. He bailed out of his upper-class Grosse Pointe high school on prom night and stood up his date, Minnie Driver, in the process. He went on to become a contract killer. How can he face the girl he stood up—with whom he's still in love? How does he explain what he does for a living? And why are people trying to kill him at his reunion? The answers to these questions await you in this quirky and appropriately deadpan comedy.

Detroit Rock City (1999)

It is the 1970s and four teenage buddies want to get to the KISS show in Detroit. Naturally, they are beset by challenges along the way. Will they make it to see their heroes in concert? KISS fans and people who were teenagers around 1977 will best appreciate this comedy, as they will be amply rewarded with in-jokes (like the fact the girls in the film are named "Beth" and "Christine," after KISS songs) and by an appearance from the band members, who play themselves 20 years earlier.

8 Mile (2002)

In this semiautobiographical film Eminem plays a scrappy kid who wants to make it big as a rapper but has to deal with the usual depressing blue-collar blues, along with a vengeful mother (Kim Basinger). It's a familiar tale, but told with twists and smarts. Eminem walked off with an Oscar for the film, although not for acting—it was for Best Song.

House of David

What do you get when you mix vegetarianism, ball games, scandals, and an amusement park with seven anointed messengers of God? The House of David, of course.

The Israelite House of David traces its roots to England, where, in 1814, Joanna Southcott announced that she was the first of Seven Messengers sent by God to save the world. Subsequent messengers adopted some unusual rules: outlawing shaving and haircutting, and enacting "blood-cleansing" rites in which messengers deflowered the flock's virgins. By the mid-1800s, these sex scandals plagued the group (by then known as the "Flying Rollers"), and they hit the road. Three separate factions were established in Australia, Canada, and Michigan.

Will the Real Seventh Messenger Please Stand Up?

The largest group landed in Detroit, led by the Seventh Messenger, Michael Mills, or Prince Mike. In 1894 Prince Mike announced that women would become communal property, to be rotated among the men. Mrs. Prince Mike sued for divorce and in the ensuing court proceedings, morals charges were leveled against Prince Mike, and he was sent to jail for five years.

With Mike in jail, a man named Benjamin Purnell stepped forward and said that he was the *real* Seventh Messenger and that Prince Mike was an imposter. Purnell garnered enough support to found the Israelite House of David in Fostoria, Ohio, in 1902. But, once a Michigander, always a Michigander. The group returned to the state after just a year in Ohio, moving to Benton Harbor, Michigan, in 1903.

Take Me Out to the Ball Game

According to the House of David Museum, the group practiced vegetarianism, celibacy, and conscientious objection to war. One way the members entertained themselves was by crafting instruments and forming bands and orchestras. The musical performances also drew attention to their street-corner preachers and was another means of income for the community.

In the early 1900s they established the Eden Springs Park amusement park—with its miniature railway, ice cream parlor, a zoo, and musical and vaudeville acts. It was a phenomenal success, selling in excess of 200,000 tickets each summer.

The House of David's baseball team also drew huge crowds. It was so good it eventually went semipro. Next, a traveling basketball team was organized in 1954, which toured Europe and even played the Harlem Globetrotters. By some estimates, the House of David earned over $10 million with these combined ventures. As the group's population aged, the teams slowly faded away.

The Fall of the House of David Empire

Now if Purnell had actually adhered to the group's celibacy

rules, everything might have been fine. But Purnell allegedly continued the "blood-cleansing" rituals with the cult's virgins— that celibacy rule was apparently just for the followers—and incurred several morals charges from 1910 to 1923. He was also accused of committing fraud and encouraging his followers to commit perjury and obstruct justice. Trials ensued up until his death in 1927. A schism in the sect developed after Purnell's death; his wife Mary finally dissolved the Israelite House of David and reorganized it into Mary's City of David in 1930.

Where Are They Now?

Mary's City of David is still a practicing religious community, though membership has flagged recently. If you're in Benton Harbor, check out Mary's City of David Museum and Tours, which brings to life the unusual history of this religious sect with documents, photographs, artifacts, and carefully restored machinery and buildings. Between May and October they also put on vintage baseball games—playing by 1858 rules.

DID YOU KNOW?

An early proponent of suffrage, preacher and educator Sojourner Truth moved to Michigan in 1857 and continued to carry on her advocacy activities. In November 1872, the fact that neither women nor African Americans were yet allowed to vote did not deter the indomitable Ms. Truth, who, at age 75, turned up at a Grand Rapids polling place and requested a ballot. She was turned away.

Baseball in Beards

*The House of David was known for many things but was
probably most noted for its baseball team, which barnstormed
across the United States from the 1920s to the 1950s. The team
was a sensation in small towns across the country. Here are
a few things Uncle John dug up about HOD baseball.*

- **The Pepper Game.** Coach Jesse Lee "Doc" Tally created a
  warm-up drill he called "pepper" that improved his players'
  speed and coordination. A pepper game consisted of at least
  three fielders standing 20 to 30 feet from the batter. The batter hit the ball to one of the fielders, who caught the ball
  quickly and lobbed it from his glove back to the batter, who
  hit the ball out to another player. The ball moved very
  quickly and the players showed off by adding a flourish to
  their moves. Fans loved the comic antics of the men in
  beards and long hair. It became so popular that it was
  moved to the fifth inning, renamed the Pepper Game, and
  billed as a mid-game exhibition.

- **Incognito.** Over the years, many big-leaguers played for the
  HOD teams, including Grover Cleveland Alexander, a Hall
  of Famer and Major League pitcher, and Negro League legend and Hall of Famer Satchel Paige. These players were

required to disguise themselves as HOD members by growing beards or wearing fake ones. (Satchel Paige wore a false red beard that didn't fool anyone.) One enduring myth claims that Babe Ruth played for HOD, but there is no proof of that. It is true, though, that HOD once made him an offer, but he never took them up on it.

- **Frequent Travelers.** Grover Cleveland Alexander once said, "If you want to see the world, join the Navy. If you want to see the United States, join the House of David baseball team." It was not unusual for the team to log more than 30,000 miles a year playing baseball across the United States.

- **Baseball Firsts.** During the 1930s the House of David team set several firsts in baseball history: They signed the first female (pitcher Jackie Mitchell) to a pro baseball contract in 1933. They played the very first night baseball game, utilizing a portable lighting system, at Riverside Park in Independence, Kansas, on April 17, 1930. And they were the first white team to regularly play teams from the Negro League, like the Kansas City Monarchs.

DID YOU KNOW?

In 2003 Golfer Dave Ladensack stunned his golf buddies when he landed not one, but two holes-in-one at the Port Huron Elks Golf Club. Odds are he won't repeat his double doozy within the next 335,000 years. Chances of pulling off such a feat are 67 million to 1, according to *Golf Digest* magazine.

Bohemian Rhapsody

*Michigan's production of commercial beer was limited to
dark English ale until the 1850s, when German immigrants
introduced golden lagers to a thirsty young nation.*

Bernhard Stroh was 26 years old when the chaos of the
German Revolution of 1848 caused him to leave home for
a German settlement first in Brazil then in the United States. In
1850 the young man was on his way to a new life in Chicago
when he stopped off at Detroit, liked what he saw, and stayed
to create a happy-hour dynasty.

The Stroh family traced their history as brewers back to
Bernhard's grandfather, who was making lager in Kirn in 1775.
Having been trained in the family's brewing trade, young Stroh
set up the Lion Brewery at 37 Catherine Street the same year
that he arrived. Pushing a two-wheeled cart through the streets
and knocking on doors, he sold a pale golden lager that he
produced at the rate of about a barrel a day.

Lager Is Good for What Ales You

Stroh's golden lager was an immediate hit with the German
immigrant community who up to then had only been able to
quench their thirst with dark English ale. Lion Brewery

expanded to meet the demand, and the crowned lion logo became well known as the symbol of Stroh's.

In 1865 Stroh bought additional land on Gratiot Avenue and expanded the brewery. By the time Bernhard died in 1882, there were 23 breweries in Detroit and over 140 in the state, but Lion Brewery was the largest of them all. At the turn of the century, it produced 50,000 barrels a year.

Changes on Tap

Not much changed until 1908, when Stroh's eldest son, Bernhard Jr., passed the mantle to younger brother Julius, who renamed the Lion as the Stroh Brewing Company. In 1912 he adopted the European "fire-brewing" process in which mash was heated in copper kettles over an open fire. The intense heat caramelized the malt sugars, giving added character. Copper kettles and open flames became both a brewing technique and an advertising hallmark of Stroh's, which billed itself as "America's only fire-brewed beer."

The company faced a new challenge in 1920, when the National Prohibition Act banned the manufacture, transportation, sale, and consumption of alcohol. Julius devised a survival strategy and began creating nonalcoholic beers and carbonated sodas rather than foaming beers. But Julius's sweetest idea was using a unit of the brewery to make ice cream. Stroh's Ice Cream became a favorite Michigan treat that's still made today under the Melody Farms label. Julius's plans succeeded, and the brewery was still around and ready to provide Detroit with plenty of suds to toast Prohibition's repeal in 1933.

Julius died in 1939 and his sons managed the company without much change, though the industry itself was changing as larger breweries went national and swallowed up the smaller, local competition. After World War II, Stroh fought with Goebel Brewery for dominance in Detroit and finally took it over in 1964. Stroh became the beer in the Motor City.

Brewing Activism

In 1968 Peter Stroh, Bernhard's great-grandson, took over the company. In 1967 he and other executives watched the smoke and flames of the Detroit riots from the brewery's roof on Gratiot. The events he witnessed convinced him that Stroh's should help give Detroit a better future. He contributed money to revitalize blighted areas of Detroit. He financed the Stroh River Place, a 26-acre site with office spaces, a restaurant, and a hotel. The city's medical center, symphony, and even the zoo all were beneficiaries of Stroh's corporate and personal largesse.

As for the business, Peter jolted the brewery into modern times with the 1978 introduction of Stroh's Light—the company's first new brew in 128 years. By 1979 Stroh's brews were sold in 17 states, and Peter was just getting warmed up. Acquisitions of New York's F. & M. Schaefer Brewing Company in 1981 and Milwaukee's Schlitz Brewing Company in 1982 made Stroh's the third largest brewery.

In 1985, to increase profitability, Peter Stroh reluctantly decided to demolish the brewery on Gratiot Avenue and move the actual brewing process to various locations out of state. In 1988 Stroh's sold 25 million barrels in the United States. Peter even took the brew overseas—to Japan in 1995 and to India in

1998. By early 1999, even though Stroh was the fourth largest brewer in the nation, the competition and falling sales forced Stroh to sell out to two rivals. Pabst Brewery in San Antonio, Texas, and Miller Brewery in Milwaukee became the new breweries for Stroh's brands of beer with Pabst producing the "lion's" share.

The state historical site marker erected in Detroit in 1976 at the old Stroh Brewery on Gratiot Avenue gives a brief history of the company. The marker has also had an interesting history of its own. In 2000 it turned up for sale on eBay. The 80-pound historical tablet had been purchased as part of an estate sale in Palm Beach, Florida. No one knew how the marker got to Florida, but eBay immediately canceled the auction because the state of Michigan considered the marker stolen property. In 2002 the state struck a deal and paid the seller $1,000. The historic marker was returned to its rightful place.

A CLOSE SHAVE

In June 2001 Dana Coldwell, 31, of Frankenmuth, was mowing her lawn when the mower blade struck a 1.5-inch-long nail and sent it hurtling toward her chest. The nail struck her on the left breast, but didn't pierce her heart—an injury that could have been fatal. Why? It was deflected by the "liquid-curved" Maidenform bust-enhancing bra she was wearing. "I almost didn't wear the bra, but a higher power told me to put it on," she says. "I don't know if I will be mowing the lawn after this, but if I do, I'll be wearing the bra."

Michigan in Song

Looking to make a Michigan-themed mixed tape or CD for a road trip through the Wolverine State? Here are some songs to get you started.

"Second Week of Deer Camp," Da Yoopers

Before the movie *Fargo* highlighted the comical eccentricities of upper Midwesterners, Da Yoopers were poking fun at themselves and Michiganders with a catalog of self-deprecating novelty songs. They even managed to find a cult audience beyond Michigan when "Second Week of Deer Camp" received frequent airplay on Dr. Demento's national radio show. Some sample lyrics: "An icy breeze is blowin', through the tongue and groove. My pants are frozen to the floor and I'm too sick to move. I didn't drink too many, only 30 cans of beer. It must have been that last shot that put me under here."

"Fred Bear," Ted Nugent

Fred Bear—the godfather of modern archery—was Michigan rocker Ted Nugent's friend and mentor, as well as a native of Grayling, Michigan. "Fred Bear" eulogizes the famous archer, and it finds Nugent stepping outside his Motor City Madman persona into the realm of contemplative introspection. The result is a sincere and likeable tribute song.

"Say Yes! to Michigan," Sufjan Stevens

Tourism officials generated the slogan "Say Yes to Michigan" in 1982 to fuel a state promotional campaign. (Yooper residents put a more northernly spin on the catch phrase, of course, transforming it into "Say Yah to Da U.P., Eh!"). More recently, indie rocker Sufjan Stevens of Holland, Michigan, turned the "Say Yes" slogan into song for his critically lauded 2003 album, *Greetings from Michigan: The Great Lakes State.*

"I Want to Go Back to Michigan (Down on the Farm)," Judy Garland

This wistful tune was featured in the movie *Easter Parade,* in which Judy Garland can be heard singing the song's Irving Berlin-penned lyrics in her portrayal of a New York City nightclub entertainer. The Andrews Sisters also performed a version of the song, as did Laurel and Hardy. And controversial filmmaker (and Davison, Michigan, native) Michael Moore featured the tune on the soundtrack to his Oscar-winning *Bowling for Columbine.*

"Faygo Boat Song," Ed Labunski (originally sung for Faygo by Kenny Karen)

In 1907 two Russian immigrant brothers founded Faygo, a Detroit soft drink company. Back in the 1950s and 60s, nearly every kid in the Detroit metro area knew the Faygo ad jingle lyrics: "Which way did he go? Which way did he go? He went for Faygo, old fashioned Root Beer." In the 1970s "Great Gildersleeve" radio star Harold Peary led Faygo's hit TV commercial jingle, "Faygo Boat Song." More recently, members of the rap group Insane Clown Posse have extolled the virtues of the Faygo nectar. (The band has guns that shoot Faygo soda into crowds at their concerts, resulting in "Faygo Frenzies.")

"Saginaw, Michigan," Lefty Frizzell

This number-one charting single crossed over from the country to the pop charts in 1964 and received a Grammy nomination. The depleted old lumber town of Saginaw is also immortalized in the songs "By the Beautiful Old Saginaw," "Saginaw, My Saginaw," Simon and Garfunkel's "America," and "There Never Was a Place Like Saginaw."

"The Wreck of the Edmund Fitzgerald," Gordon Lightfoot

The *S.S. Edmund Fitzgerald* and its crew of 29 men sunk to the bottom of Lake Superior in November 1975, inspiring this 1970s song with lyrics that give a poetic air to the tragedy.

"The Day Ted Nugent Killed All the Animals," Wally Pleasant

East Lansing's Pleasant is also a beneficiary of Dr. Demento's playlist. This song was featured on Demento's "Hunting Hit Parade." Its title assumes the listener is aware of Nugent's passion for predatory blood sports. In 1994 "Alternateen" was also a regional hit for Pleasant, who has penned songs about grandmas with bingo addictions and late nights at Denny's. A press photo for Pleasant features the tunesmith reading *Know Your Fish*.

"Hiawatha," Laurie Anderson

A spoken excerpt of Longfellow's epic poem "Song of Hiawatha" (set on the shore of Lake Superior) can be found on her 1989 album, *Strange Angels*.

Digging the Dunes

Along the shores of the Great Lakes lie 285,000 acres of a natural wonder, the freshwater coastal dunes. With 3,177 miles of shoreline, (the most of any state), Michigan has the largest expanse of the Great Lakes coastal sand dunes—an area so enormous it can be seen from space!

Michigan's shores are blessed with plenty of rainfall—too much according to some soaked natives. Most people think of dunes as being located in the hot, dry desert. So why have so many dunes formed in wet and wild Michigan? A Chippewa-Ojibway legend offers one explanation for the presence of the dunes in Sleeping Bear Dunes National Lakeshore: A mother bear and her cubs swam across Lake Michigan to escape a forest fire. The mother made it to land but could not find her cubs, so she climbed to the top of a hill to watch for them. The mother bear fell asleep waiting for her cubs, and the sands covered her, forming a dune. The scientific explanation isn't quite as romantic.

Drifting into Michigan

Over a million years ago, glaciers began digging out the Great Lakes. The last great ice sheet, the Wisconsin Glacier, covered Michigan under heavy ice about a mile thick. Pushing down on the earth and moving slowly, the glacier scraped up a mass of boulders and pebbles called "glacial drift." The ice floe ground some of the drift into grit and dust, leaving some particles the size of sand. As the climate warmed, the glaciers melted and left the glacial drift behind—including sand and rock particles that slowly eroded into sand.

How to Grow a Dune

Michigan's coastal dunes have been formed in the last 10,000 years. The glacial ice sheets brought plenty of sand, and erosion created more. When the ice melted, sand was redeposited in river basins and lakeshores.

Winds also moved the sands around until they met obstructions like cliffs. Plants, trees, or heavier rocks trapped the deposited sands. Over thousands of years sands dumped, trapped, and stablized by rainfall formed dunes.

The sand dunes near Lake Michigan are named for their locations. The beach dunes have developed along the lake's low-lying shores. The inland dunes have formed some distance from the lake (where lakeshores once existed thousands of years ago). High above are the perched dunes, so called because they perch on ridges, or "moraines," formed by the glaciers. The Sleeping Bear Dune is a perched dune rising 200 feet above Lake Michigan. Perched dunes are a stunning sight—mountains of sand looming above the lake.

Quartz and Quartz of Sand

Michigan dunes are 90 percent quartz. The uniform quartz particles result in a fine sand with an almost silken feel when run through one's fingers or toes. No sandpaper feeling here, since about 1850 the dunes have been mined for sand to use in industry. In the mid-1800s dune sand was mined for use in iron foundries. Today over 90 percent of dune sand is still mined for foundries to make molds and cores. The rest of the sand is typically mined for products like glass and concrete.

Modern Michigan industries and foundries prize dune sand for its uniformity, its high silica content, its small particles, and its ability to withstand high heat. After some massive dunes were lost, the state of Michigan passed the Dune Protection Act in 1976, but environmentalists claim the act has too many loopholes and dunes are being destroyed. They have called for a ban on mining in the dunes by 2006. Industry representatives maintain that responsible mining can coexist with preserving the most environmentally sensitive dunes.

In the meantime, the dunes themselves keep changing. Some dunes migrate, pushed along by the wind. The sand has been known to bury trees and then move on beyond them, leaving behind dead, dune-destroyed "ghost forests." Dunes can collapse too. In 1995 George Weeks was walking his dog along the shore in Sleeping Bear Dunes National Lakeshore, when he saw that part of his usual path had become a 100-foot drop into Lake Michigan. A landslide had sent the dunes and part of the bluff into the lake.

Controversial, ever-changing, and spectacular, the dunes are the Ice Age's gift to Michigan. As Carl Sandburg once put it, they "constitute a signature of time and eternity."

Hometown:
A Touch of Dutch

*This picture-perfect community boasts an authentic Dutch culture
that has prospered since its founding.*

Town: Holland
Location: Ottawa and Allegan counties
Founding: 1847
Current population: 35,000 (est.)
Size: 17 square miles

What's in a Name?

When a small group of Dutch Calvinist separatists settled the
area in 1847, "Holland" was both a logical and nostalgic choice
for the town's name.

Claim to Fame:

- Begun in 1929 at the suggestion of a Holland High teacher, the
  week-long Tulip Time Festival boasts more than 6 million fully
  bloomed tulips and other perennials along an eight-mile
  stretch of land. The festival brings thousands of visitors each
  May. But visitors beware: picking a tulip results in a $50 fine!

- The 240-year-old DeZwaan windmill, located in the center of 35-acre Windmill Island, was brought from the Netherlands to Holland in 1964. Today it is a fully functioning windmill that grinds wheat into flour. The 12-story DeZwaan (meaning "the swan") is the only authentic Dutch windmill in the United States. After DeZwaan was brought to the United States, the Dutch government stopped allowing windmills to be removed from the Netherlands.

- The town is home to the only wooden shoe factory in North America and the only blue and white delftware factory in the United States. Visitors are allowed to watch the shoe-making and china-making processes from start to finish in the DeKlomp Wooden Shoe and Delftware Factory.

- Holland is also home to Heinz, USA, the world's largest pickle factory, where up to one million pickles are processed every day.

- Holland has both great beaches in summer as well as great skiing in winter. If you want to avoid the cold white stuff, the downtown area has 60 miles of tubing under its streets through which flows recycled warm water to keep the area snowfree.

KLOMPEN WISDOM

A rich man lived to skimp and save, a poor man only spent and gave. Each wears but two klompen in his grave!

A son follows his father's klompen, not his words.

Ghostly Girls

Legend has it that Mackinac Island's Arch Rock was formed by a Native American maiden's tears that washed away the limestone bluff as she waited in vain for her lover's return. But other legends tell of specters who haunt Michigan. Find out if there might be a ghost in your neighborhood.

The Hidden Beauty

Chief Sleeping Bear of the Ottawa tribe had a daughter so stunning that he hid her in a covered canoe tied to a tree on the bank of the Detroit River. One day, when he brought her food, the wind caught a glimpse of her and was enchanted by her beauty. After the father's departure, the wind tried to blow the canoe's cover off, but the rope snapped and the canoe floated downriver toward Lake Huron. When the keeper of the lake's water gates saw the girl, he, too, was captivated. He gave chase and brought her back to be his wife. Angry at the keeper's interference, the winds beat him to death. They also smashed the girl's boat, which magically became an island on which the girl climbed to safety. The winds confessed their deeds to Chief Sleeping Bear and begged him not to hide his daughter from them. The chief agreed, but asked the Great Spirit to surround the island with snakes to deter intruders.

Until colonization by the French, the island was known as

Wah-na-be-zee (Swan Island) to the resident Chippewa and Ottawa tribes. Early settlers renamed it Isle St. Clair, but soon changed the name more fittingly to Rattlesnake Island. Next it was renamed Belle Isle. Located northeast of Detroit, the island has a large park, zoo, and botanical garden. Picnickers have reported encountering a beautiful white doe that, when approached, transforms into a beautiful Indian maiden.

The Bickering Sisters

In the early 1700s the Wyandot tribe lived on the banks of the Detroit River, near the city of Wyandotte, between what is now Oak Street and Eureka Avenue. One chief had three beautiful daughters who would not stop arguing. The girls' reputations for quarreling spread to neighboring tribes. As a result, their father was unable to find them husbands. But even this did not stop the sisters, who bickered so much and were so difficult to get along with that even the women of the tribe avoided them.

To restore peace to the village, the chief moved his daughters to separate wigwams far away from the tribe. But they continued to argue loudly and disturb the community. Unable to stand it any longer, the chief put each sister on one of three islands in the middle of Lake Erie. When the sisters could no longer quarrel with one another, they began to scream and cry. They sobbed and wailed until all three died of grief. The islands became known as the Sister Isles. To this day, they remain uninhabited. And even death may have failed to silence the sisters. Boaters that pass by claim the sisters' cries can still be heard. Others insist the sound is only the wind.

One-Sided Love

In the mid-1700s the owner of a Detroit mill, which stood at the foot of what is now 24th Street in Detroit, adopted a young Pontiac girl with the tribe's consent. As the girl grew older, one of the Pontiac warriors, Wasson, fell deeply in love with her. His tribe members advised him to forget about her.

Wasson, however, decided to spy on the girl. To his dismay, he soon discovered that she had a secret lover. Whenever her father went away, the girl would light a candle in the mill's window. Soon afterward, a figure in a military cloak would appear, knock at the door, and enter.

After many nights, Wasson identified the man as Colonel Campbell, an English officer. One night Wasson quietly crept into the girl's room through an open window and killed her with his hatchet. If he couldn't have her, no one would. Later, he killed her lover as well.

But her death did not erase her presence. After the young woman's murder, people who passed by the mill often claimed that they saw a young maiden walking with a candle in her hand, apparently in search of her lover. She frightened so many people that the mill was torn down in 1795. Even this may not have rid the town of her spirit. Some locals claim that to this day the maiden's flickering candle can still be seen along the nearby waterfront.

End of an Era

Bennett Park, the first structure to house the Detroit Tigers,
was an 8,000-seat venue that hosted Tiger games from 1896 to
1911. Owner Frank Navin tore down the structure and built Navin
Field on the site at the corner of Michigan and Trumbull avenues
in 1911; it was open for business the following year. The ballpark's
name was changed to Briggs Stadium (for new owner Walter Briggs)
in 1938 and to Tiger Stadium in 1961. This name would last
until the final game was played on September 27, 1999.

Save the Park!

Though fans cherished Tiger Stadium, in the late 1980s owner
Tom Monaghan decided it was beyond repair, citing the need
for luxury boxes and new offices that the old building could
not accommodate. The Tiger Stadium Fan Club arose to challenge the move. Fan club members John and Judy Davids, both
architects, submitted the Cochrane Plan, a detailed proposal
that showed affordable ways to integrate all the changes that
the ownership wanted without interfering with the team's
schedule or eliminating the 11,000 low-priced bleacher seats.

But the Tigers' management and the town proceeded with
the construction of Comerica Park, which opened in 2000.
Tiger Stadium still stands, though it is rarely used and the City
of Detroit is considering razing it.

Tiger Stadium By the Numbers

404: The smallest crowd in stadium history, recorded for a September 25, 1928, game against the Boston Red Sox.

104: Number of years the Tigers played baseball at the site.

11–0: Final score, Game 7 of the 1934 World Series. The Tigers lost to the St. Louis Cardinals. In the bottom of the sixth, with the Tigers trailing 9–0, frustrated fans pelted Cardinal outfielder Ducky Medwick with garbage and the baseball commissioner removed him from the game for his safety.

7/8/41: Date of the first All-Star Game at the stadium. The American League won 7–5 over the National League.

58,369: Largest crowd in stadium history. The fans were on hand for a July 20, 1947, doubleheader against the Yankees.

0: Number of hits the Tigers managed off of Cleveland's Bob Lemon on June 30, 1948. It was the first night game no-hitter in the history of the American League.

643 feet: Distance of Mickey Mantle's September 10, 1960, home run at the stadium—the longest ever measured.

626 feet: Longest home run in Babe Ruth's career, hit at the stadium on June 8, 1926.

2: Number of hits given up by Mark Fidrych in his first Major League start. He earned a 2–1 victory over Cleveland on May 15, 1976.

5: Number of World Series played at the stadium.

3: Number of All-Star Games played at the stadium.

I Want My M(ichigan) TV!

Test your knowledge of TV shows set in the Wolverine state.

Michigan has had its share of television shows set within its boundaries. We've collected some of these hits and misses to test your memory.

1. "Home Improvement" (1991–1999, ABC) was about the adventures of a klutzy TV show host (Tim Allen), as he navigated life with his wife and their three kids. What city was it set in?
   - A. Kalamazoo
   - B. Detroit
   - C. Flint

2. The 1977 CBS drama "The Fitzpatricks" about a blue-collar Michigan family, included which future Oscar-winning celebrity as part of its cast?
   - A. Marisa Tomei, as the tomboy daughter Keely Fitzpatrick
   - B. Helen Hunt, as neighborhood kid Kerry Gerardi
   - C. Geena Davis, as sexy coworker Louise Abbadano

3. The TV show "Soul Man" (1997, ABC) was:
   A. A drama about the early days of a Motown-like record label and its chief, Oswald "Ossie" Parks (actual former Motown great Lamont Dozier).
   B. A supernatural drama about a Detroit preacher (Lou Gossett Jr.) whose brush with death reveals a power to see souls, which he uses to help people in need.
   C. A comedy about a widowed preacher (Dan Aykroyd) trying to deal with four children and his parishioners in the Detroit suburbs.

4. In 2003 VH-1 broadcast a reality series in which contestants had to match wits with Motor City Madman, bowhunter, and rock legend Ted Nugent. Which one of the following facts about "Surviving Nugent" is true?
   A. Ted Nugent's ranch, the site where the show was filmed, is in Texas.
   B. At one point during the show, the famously carnivorous Nugent concedes the moral superiority of vegetarianism.
   C. The show planned to feature members of Nugent's past bands (the Amboy Dukes and Damn Yankees), but this idea was dropped when Damn Yankees member Jack Blades backed out, citing exhaustion.

5. Which of the following legal issues plagued the popular Detroit-based Fox comedy "Martin" in its final season?
   A. Costar Thomas Ford sued the *Star* for reporting that he had entered rehab after crashing his car into his garage, while the garage door was closed.

B. Star Martin Lawrence sued Fox on the grounds that repeated "off-schedule" reruns of the show were making it more difficult to syndicate the series.

C. Costar Tisha Campbell filed charges against star Martin Lawrence for sexual harassment and walked off the show.

6. In 1999–2000, NBC aired "Freaks and Geeks," a cult-fave Michigan high school drama/comedy. Which of the following is *not* true?

A. The show was so popular at Oberlin College in Ohio that when it was canceled the school called in extra psychological counselors to help fans cope with the loss.

B. Two of the actors have gone on to costar in two film series that between them have grossed over $2 billion.

C. The DVD release of the show includes commentary from parents of cast members and also obsessive fans.

For answers, turn to page 301.

DID YOU KNOW?

Actor Jeff Daniels owns the Purple Rose Theatre in Chelsea, which he named after Woody Allen's movie, *The Purple Rose of Cairo*, in which he starred.

Bowled Over

*On a dusty field in Palo Alto, California, on January 1, 1902, the
University of Michigan Wolverines opposed the Stanford University
Cardinals in the first Rose Bowl game. In the process, they nearly
changed the way generations of sports fans would spend New Year's Day.*

The Tournament of Roses began in 1891 as a way to promote the warm winter climate of Pasadena, California, and
to attract real estate investors from the snowy East. From its
inception, sporting events were an important part of the festival, but such contests as ostrich racing, broncobusting, tug-of-
wars, and medieval jousts failed to capture the nation's attention as city fathers had hoped. So in 1901 tournament officials
decided to invite two top college football teams, one from the
East and one from the West, to face off in a "Rose Bowl."

Clash of the Titans

Choosing the teams was easy. The University of Michigan
Wolverines had dominated college football in the Midwest. The
Wolverine defense played the entire 1901 season without
allowing a single point. The Wolverine's offense average of 50
points per game caused shell-shocked opponents to call
Michigan the "Point-a-Minute" team. UM halfback Willie
Heston was one of the sport's first great stars. In a time

dominated by traditional East Coast football powers, such as Harvard and Yale, Michigan put Midwest football on the map. Many experts of the day ranked the Wolverines as the best team in the nation.

Michigan was an obvious choice to represent the East. Stanford University of Palo Alto, California, was chosen to oppose the powerful Wolverines. The Stanford Cardinals had lost only one game the previous season and were expected to uphold the honor of West Coast football.

The first Rose Bowl game kicked off at 3 p.m. on January 1, 1902. About 8,000 fans crowded onto a wooden grandstand erected on a dry and dusty Pasadena field. Those hoping for a Stanford victory were encouraged by their team's first-quarter performance; Stanford held Michigan scoreless. But by halftime Heston and his teammates led 17–0. The rout continued in the second half. Finally, with ten minutes left in the game, and Michigan leading 49–0, the exhausted and embarrassed Stanford captain admitted defeat and the game was called.

Tournament organizers were appalled; even broncobusting had been more competitive, the West Coast favorites had been beaten, and the fans had not seen an entire game. Thinking that college football was not such a great attraction after all, they decided to replace it with gladiator-style chariot races. For the next ten years, the chariot races attracted big crowds to the festival and seemed poised to become a new sporting national pastime, until a bad accident resulted in their cancellation. By 1916 college football had secured its place as one of the most popular sports in the country, and tournament officials decided to give it another chance. This time it was successful and football became an annual festival highlight, rivaling even the parade in popular appeal. Eventually other bowl games were held, but the Rose Bowl was the granddaddy of them all.

A Michigan team would not return to the Rose Bowl until 1948 when, ironically, the Wolverines defeated the University of Southern California by the same 49–0 score of the first Rose Bowl game.

DID YOU KNOW?

- The Eastern Michigan University College of Education produces more classroom teachers than any other school.

- The "Paul Is Dead" hoax that haunted the Beatles in 1969 became a phenomenon when Russ Gibb, an Eastern Michigan University student working at WKNR-FM, began airing "clues" to Paul's death on his radio program.

- The male/female ratio at Michigan Tech is 3:1. To improve the ratio, the school began offering a philosophy major in 2004.

- The book *Fire Ants*, by Saginaw Valley State University assistant professor Stephen Taber, was featured in the 2005 "CSI" season finale. Investigator Grissom uses it to solve a crime.

- In the early 1940s Western Michigan University granted graduate degrees through the University of Michigan. Courses were taken at WMU, but UM professors supervised them.

- The Superior Dome, a sports stadium at Northern Michigan University, had the world's highest wooden dome when it was built in 1991.

Hoop Magic

*Earvin "Magic" Johnson is famous for bringing a
fast-paced offense called "Showtime" to the Lakers' Los Angeles
Forum, and for pulling millions of new fans into the National
Basketball Association. But before that, young Earvin was
making hoop fanatics out of his Lansing neighbors. And
Lansing was making its mark on Magic*

The Magic Secret

Born in 1959, Earvin and his six brothers and sisters lived in
a small house at 814 Middle Street. Magic found the black,
working-class neighborhood "a great place to grow up." The
Johnsons were a close, hardworking family, with Earvin Sr.
always balancing a second job in addition to his shift on the
General Motors assembly line, while Earvin's mom, Christine,
worked in the school cafeteria. The kids pitched in, including
young Earvin, who helped his dad clean office buildings, did
chores for mom, and mowed neighborhood lawns for extra
money. When Earvin got a chance, he shot hoops at a local
court. The Johnson work ethic showed up in young Earvin's
serious drill on his basketball skills. Earvin Johnson considered constant practice his "magic" secret.

Lansing Got Game

In 1974 Lansing residents began taking notice of a tall (eventually 6 feet 9 inches) kid playing for Dwight Rich Junior High. With Earvin on their team, Dwight Rich had an unstoppable winning steak. But when Earvin entered high school, everyone assumed his winning days were over. The Everett Vikings were picked to finish dead last in basketball. When Johnson joined the team, he contributed enthusiasm and the hard work necessary to improve his game. When his teammates followed his lead, Everett began to win! Fred Stabley Jr., sportswriter for the *Lansing State Journal,* watched 15-year-old Earvin score 36 points and grab 18 rebounds at a high school game and dubbed him "Magic." The new moniker fit and stuck as the Vikings made it to the state semifinals in 1976 and won their first regional championship in 1977.

The Birdman vs. the Magic Man

By now Magic was a local hero. Michigan's sports pages were filled with speculation about where Magic Johnson would play college ball. All of Lansing wanted Magic to wear the green-and-white Spartan uniform of hometown university Michigan State. When Magic finally announced that he was "born to be a Spartan," Lansing residents went wild.

Once poorly attended MSU basketball games soon had crowded bleachers. Everyone came to watch the fast breaks and creative passing that Magic used to launch the ball to his teammate Greg Kelser, who then dunked it in the basket. Under the direction of Coach Jud Heathcoate, Magic and Kelser launched an early version of the great passing game that would later be known as "Showtime." They lit up the scoreboard and in 1978 the Spartans won their first Big Ten Conference title in 19 years. The following year they were the regional champions, playing in the annual NCAA tournament.

In the final game of the 1979 tournament Michigan State was pitted against undefeated Indiana State. Millions tuned in to see the joust between Magic and Indiana State's superstar, Larry Bird. The Spartans formulated a defense against the powerful "Birdman," and the team practiced it cold. The result was a 75–64 victory over Indiana and a personal victory for Magic, who won the Most Valuable Player award in the tournament. That game drew a 24.1 rating, one of the highest ever for collegiate basketball.

Life After Basketball

By 1980 Magic had left college to turn pro when he was drafted by the Los Angeles Lakers. Magic led his team to five championships, earning the Most Valuable Player award three times.

In September 1991 Magic returned briefly to Lansing to marry his MSU freshman sweetheart, Earletha "Cookie" Johnson. Less than two months later, he held a press conference to announce to a stunned and saddened nation that he would be retiring from basketball because he had HIV, which can cause AIDS.

Over a decade later, Magic has stayed healthy. He speaks publicly about the need for safe sex to prevent AIDS. And he is now a CEO—a career that he had actually mapped out as a kid when he did janitorial work cleaning the offices of Lansing's top businessmen. Johnson Development Corporation is a multimillion-dollar company headquartered in Los Angeles. Magic partners with chains like Starbucks and T.G.I. Friday's to bring business to neglected urban areas. Johnson has brought a Starbucks and muliplex to Detroit. In 1999 Johnson attended the grand opening of a Starbucks he bought on Grand River Avenue in East Lansing. Signed jerseys from his high school, college, and professional career adorn the walls.

DID YOU KNOW?

Before he was "Magic," Earvin Johnson had another nickname. When he was very young, his neighbors called the chubby youngster "June Bug" because he was round like the June bug beetle (common in the Great Lakes area). And like a frantic June bug, Earvin bounced around the neighborhood, dribbling a basketball and looking for a place to shoot hoops.

Young Earvin did not like the undignified name, and he was glad when he grew taller and the name faded into the past. But at some point, he must have changed his mind because in 2004, Johnson launched a line of athletic clothing and footwear as part of a new company called June Bug Enterprises.

A Spooky De-Light

*Strange lights have appeared at nightfall in an isolated
forest between Watersmeet and Paulding in the Upper Peninsula
for over a hundred years. "Ripley's Believe It or Not" offered more
than $100,000 to anyone who could solve the mystery, but
no one was able to claim the prize.*

The Paulding Lights are such a popular tourist attraction
that the Michigan Forest Service has put up markers pointing out the best viewing areas. Described as ranging in shape
from circles to octagons, stars, diamonds, and spinning wheels,
and in color from white to red, yellow, and green, the lights
seem to dance and jump near the horizon. Some observers
claim that they seem intelligent—teasing and beckoning
onlookers, and sometimes approaching to within a few feet.
The lights seem to prefer quiet because on nights when visitors
are too noisy, they disappear.

Supernatural Theories

- The lights seem to appear where a railroad line once serv-
  iced a lumber camp. Many people believe that the lights
  stem from a terrible train wreck that occurred there, and
  where power lines are still visible. Though several theories

seek to explain the mysterious lights, the following three involve a lantern:

Version #1: The ghost of a brakeman, angry at his demise in the wreck, waves his lantern to warn others of the danger.

Version #2: The train's engineer, responsible for the mishap, waves his lantern as he searches for his soul.

Version #3: The lantern belongs to a pair of siblings who were on the ill-fated train. The sister was decapitated in the accident and now her brother waves a lantern while looking for her head.

- Some believe that the lights represent the souls of Native American braves who died in battle.

- Ecologically minded believers maintain that the lights represent the ghost of a Native American chief perched in protest upon the power lines that "defiled" the area.

- Then there's the story of Pancake Joe, the owner of a pool hall in neighboring Watersmeet. His life was ruined when the power lines were erected (just how is not entirely clear). In protest, he climbs the power lines each night, setting off sparks and frightening people away.

- Some believe that the spot is a portal for communication with the netherworld.

- And, of course, others insist that aliens are responsible and/or that UFOs cause the lights.

Let's Hear It for Science

Others try to provide the following rational explanations for the lights:

- Car headlights

- Swamp gas, formed by decaying matter, that has taken on a gaseous, luminescent form

- Reflections from Lake Superior

Critics of any scientific explanation like to point out that the lights were reported before cars existed, the area has no swamps, and no other lights of this kind have been spotted bouncing off the other lakes.

The most interesting observation regarding the lights, rendered by an anonymous long-time resident in the area: "The longer visitors linger in the nearby bar, the brighter the lights seem to be!"

DID YOU KNOW?

With place names like Copper Harbor, Ironwood, Rockland, Agate Falls Park, and Crystal Falls, it is not surprising that the Upper Peninsula is a rock hound's paradise. Over 100 minerals, from agates to copper to hematite to quartz, can be found in the area. Generally rock collecting on public lands is free, but often there are regulations to follow, so check with a local rock shop before digging in.

Celebrity Michigan

Whether they're actors, singers, writers, comedians, athletes, or captains of industry, there's no shortage of famous folk from the Wolverine State. You'll find 28 of them here—a mere fraction of the state's dozens of celebrated offspring.

NELSON ALGREN	ED MCMAHON
SONNY BONO	ROSA PARKS
BRUCE CATTON	DELLA REESE
TY COBB	SUGAR RAY ROBINSON
EDNA FERBER	DIANA ROSS
GERALD R FORD	EERO SAARINEN
HENRY FORD	STEVEN SEAGAL
EDGAR GUEST	BOB SEGER
GORDIE HOWE	TOM SELLECK
LEE IACOCCA	MARLO THOMAS
CASEY KASEM	LILY TOMLIN
PIPER LAURIE	ROBERT WAGNER
JOE LOUIS	SERENA WILLIAMS
MADONNA	STEVIE WONDER

```
N A D F O L N R E O K L E D D A D A N O
I M I N G P C A R E A O I E O R A Y A R
L B A E B E I O N O B Y N N O S D L A E
M C N D B L H P R E B R E F A N D E D G
O A A S O C L E E N Y O R R O N E M S E
T S R E C N D L N R R D S T M D C O S S
Y E O R Y N N M A R L O T H O M A S K B
L Y S E T R A A L A Y A L O A A A D R O
I K S N E R G F R N C F U H H G N E A B
L A G A E S N E V E T S O R B I D L P O
S S O W R L G L C E D N U R I T W L A I
I E E I O S S U L L M N O E D E D A S C
U M E L S S R O D T E W O H E I D R O G
O E B L A B E R N A E Y D W D P R E R R
L E E I A C O C C A T O M S E L L E C K
E D G A R G U E S T L E N E O I M S E A
O V R M I L A L E E D G D O H B V E S A
J N O S N I B O R Y A R R A G U S E V E
B R O B E R T W A G N E R E D R S S T L
E O R F N N A S S A I O L A N O E E S S
```

For answers, turn to page 301.

Pick a Pocket

*From its humble beginnings on the end of a miner's
shovel to its current status as a popular Upper Peninsula
export, the pasty is a signature Michigan taste.*

Pasties are rooted in the history of Michigan's Upper
Peninsula copper and iron mines. In the early to mid-1800s,
the mines were expanded so quickly that their owners began to
look abroad for suitable labor. The miners of Cornwall,
England, were perfect recruits because of their experience in
that region's tin and copper deposits. The Cornish mines
required working underground to extract minerals from hard
rock, similar to the conditions in the U.P. mines. The rise of
Michigan's mining industry also came at just the right time.
The industry in Cornwall was near collapse, and the unem-
ployed miners were eager to cross the Atlantic in pursuit of a
steady paycheck.

The Cornish miners would have become just another
thread in the immigrant tapestry of 19th-century America if it
weren't for one thing—their lunches. Every morning their
wives would send them off to work with baked pasties—folded
over piecrust pockets filled with vegetables and meat. The
pasties' portability was important for workers who remained

underground all day. The crimped edges of the crust made a convenient handle, and miners could easily eat the filling and dispose of any crust they dirtied with their hands. When it was time for lunch, a miner would stop work, set his pasty on a shovel, and heat it over the candles from his headlamp. The warm and filling meal provided much-needed nourishment for a hard day of mining.

Although the Cornish were not the only immigrant group working the mines, they were by far the most experienced, a fact that other miners quickly noticed. Finnish and Swedish miners soon copied Cornish mining methods along with the favorite Cornish lunch. While the Cornish and Swedish immigrant communities died out with the closing of the mines in the early 20th century, descendants of the Finnish miners remained. Had the Finnish not adopted the pasty tradition, Cornish history in Michigan may have ended with the mines.

Pasty Particulars

Pasties maintain their half-circle pocket shape and typically average six inches across, more out of tradition than for any practical reason. Pasties enclose a meet filling of beef and/or pork, complemented by some variation of potatoes, onions, rutabagas or turnips, carrots, and rhubarb. While the original Cornish cooks used sliced meat, Finns later changed the recipe to use diced meat. Beef gravy is now an essential dipping sauce, although ketchup is also an old standby, but it is perfectly acceptable to eat a pasty plain. You can expect to spend three to five dollars on a pasty, depending on the quality and the ingredients. It's important to note that the proper pronunciation of pasty is PASS-tee rather than PAYS-tee.

As you near the Mackinac Bridge, large hand-painted signs for "Homemade Pasties" beckon locals and tourists alike to family-owned shops and restaurants throughout the U.P. You can stop for lunch and stock the cooler for the trip home, but you need not worry about buying enough to last until your next trip up north. Albie's Pasties carries the legacy throughout Michigan with frozen pasties available at most grocery stores. If you crave homemade pasties, you can find them at fairs and festivals that recognize the food's proven money-making ability. For those outside of Michigan, the residents of Still Waters Community Elders Home in the U.P. town of Calumet have you covered. Through their Web site they deliver homemade pasties anywhere in the United States.

Whether you buy pasties on the way home from work or have them shipped from thousands of miles away, pass the gravy and try a bite of this historic and compact meal.

HOTDOG RIVALS

Looking for a good hotdog? Try Lafayette Coney Island and American Coney Island in Detroit. Located side by side, these two restaurants have been serving their chili- and onion-smothered Coney dogs for 70-plus years now. Owned by the families of two immigrant brothers who originally opened the restaurants, the friendly rivalry has become a sort of turf war for Detroiters, who at early ages pledge allegiance to one or the other.

Michigan Rocks!

*There's more to Michigan's musical heritage than Motown.
Here are some of Michigan's best rock and rollers.*

Alice Cooper

Detroit native and lead singer Vincent Furnier fronted the
hard rock band Alice Cooper. It released its first album in
1969, but didn't really take off until the Los Angeles–based
band moved to Detroit and honed its over-the-top live act,
which featured lots of mascara and theatrical touches like on-
stage guillotines. Its biggest year was 1972, when "School's
Out" became a huge hit.

Eminem

Eminem was a part-time Michigander, shuttling between the
Detroit suburbs and Missouri as a child, but has become
strongly identified with Detroit, especially since the release of
the film *8 Mile,* which takes its name from a Detroit street.
Eminem's raunchy lyrics in his first two albums, *The Slim
Shady LP* and *The Marshall Mathers LP,* have caused people to
accuse him of misogyny and homophobia; Eminem responded
by performing his hit "Stan" at the Grammys with openly gay
rock icon Elton John.

Grand Funk Railroad

In the early 1970s Grand Funk Railroad was the band that critics loved to hate. The Flint-based band played meat-and-potatoes rock that was perfect for rides in muscle cars and summer yard parties. This didn't stop Grand Funk from selling more records in 1970 than any other American band or from selling out a Shea Stadium concert in record time.

Iggy Pop & the Stooges

Considered by many to be one of the two most influential rock bands out of Michigan (the other being MC5), the Stooges, whose raw, anarchic style presaged punk by almost a decade, debuted in Ann Arbor in 1967. They released albums in 1969 and 1970 before the band broke up because of Iggy Pop's drug problems. Rocker David Bowie rode to the rescue and got the band back together for 1973's seminal *Raw Power* album, which Bowie coproduced, but drugs broke up the band again.

Kid Rock

Kid Rock is the evolutionary link between hard rock and rap. The Romeo native's first album, *Grit Sandwiches for Breakfast* (1990), was roundly ignored, but Rock's potent combination of southern-fried hard rock and white-boy rap crossed over into the national consciousness with 1998's multiplatinum *Devil Without a Cause.*

MC5

This band influenced punk with its uncompromising, serrated rock music and its lifestyle. The "house band" of the "White

Panthers," an anarchic/revolutionary group founded by band manager John Sinclair, the group appeared at various political gatherings including Abbie Hoffman's "yippie" rally at Chicago's ill-fated 1968 Democratic convention. The profanity-laced band's 1969 debut album, *Kick Out the Jams,* was banned at Hudson's department stores. Sinclair roasted the store in his counterculture magazine *Fifth Estate,* and Hudson's responded by yanking all the albums produced by Elektra, the band's label. A band this revolutionary could not last, and this one did not, breaking up in 1972.

Ted Nugent

The "Motor City Madman" has been a rock and roll audience favorite since his days with the Amboy Dukes in the late sixties, but it was with his self-titled band that Nugent let loose, prowling around the stage dressed as a caveman and serving up slice after bloody slice of red-meat rock and roll. Famously straight-edged (he claims not to drink or indulge in drugs), Nugent has cultivated a controversial reputation as an unapologetic conservative, a bowhunting enthusiast, and a gun ownership–rights crusader. He also maintains a side business selling hunting accessories and hunting tours.

Mitch Ryder & the Detroit Wheels

Every big city has a locally famous musician who just missed the big time: Mitch Ryder was Detroit's. Ryder (William S. Levise Jr.) and the Detroit Wheels (James McCarty, Joseph Cubert, Earl Elliot, and Johnny "Bee" Badanjek) tasted national success in 1966 with the blue-eyed soul of their top-ten hit

"Jenny Take a Ride," followed by the top-five "Devil with a Blue Dress On/Good Golly Miss Molly." Then Ryder fiddled with a good thing and went solo, to little effect; a later reunion with Wheels member Badanjek would similarly lack momentum. Ryder retired in 1973 but resurfaced and later found greater success abroad than at home.

Bob Seger

As Bruce Springsteen is to New Jersey and John Mellencamp is to Indiana, so is Bob Seger to Michigan: a homegrown, hardworking rocker with blue-collar, mid-American appeal. Seger, however, predates both of those musicians, with his 1969 album, *Ramblin' Gamblin' Man*. But Seger's national fame did not hit until he formed the Silver Bullet Band in 1974 and started unspooling a series of hits that began with "Katmandu" in 1975 and continued through the 1980s. (A now-classic placement of his song "Old Time Rock & Roll" in the film *Risky Business* did not hurt either.) Ironically, one of Seger's best-known songs is "Like a Rock," featured prominently in ads for Chevrolet trucks for over a decade. Seger was inducted into the Rock and Roll Hall of Fame in 2004.

The White Stripes

Divorced couple Jack and Meg White formed a band in 1997 and spent a few years building their indie cred (opening for bands like Sleater-Kinney and Pavement) before gaining critical and popular success in 2001 with *White Blood Cells*. Their highly regarded follow-up, *Elephant,* won some Grammys, including one for Best Rock Song for "Seven Nation Army."

Four Flags

Niles, Michigan, was claimed by four sovereign nations—France, England, Spain, and the United States—and that doesn't include the Native American tribes who called it home. What made Niles so desirable?

Long before the French arrived in 1690, Native Americans had made the St. Joseph River area their home for thousands of years, living on the land's rich abundance. Of the many tribes to pass through, the Potawatomi and Miami more than any other called it home. When the French and British arrived to fight over the area's bountiful resources, the various tribes took sides and fought among themselves and with the Europeans.

In 1691 French explorers established Fort St. Joseph on the west bank of the river by that name and raised their flag—the first to fly over the area. The site at the intersection of the river and the Native American route known as the Great Sauk Trail gave them command of the river, which provided a natural barrier against attackers and allowed fast inexpensive transportation to Lake Michigan for the export of furs to France.

As long-standing allies against the Iroquois, the French and Potawatomi got along well. The French provided protection, and in return the Potawatomi provided furs. Together, they protected their commercial venture against their mutual enemies, the Iroquois and the English. But the British were not the only problem.

The French and Potawatomi fended off the Fox and Sauk tribes seeking a share of the lucrative fur trade. During the Fox Wars, about 1712, the fort closed, although a few brave souls remained. But the fighting took its toll, leaving the fort in a weakened defensive position.

The British Are Coming!

When New France (Canada) fell to England, the British 60th regiment, called the Royal Americans, took over Fort St. Joseph in 1761. They lowered the French flag and raised their own, the second to fly over the fort. But their conquest lasted only a short time and was fraught with wars.

While the French made allies of the Native Americans, the British took a more arrogant tack. They aroused resentment by allowing white settlers to build on Native American–owned land, and eventually, the tribes united and, led by Chief Pontiac, rebelled. Although Pontiac's Rebellion was defeated, the English soldiers stationed at Fort St. Joseph had been overpowered and killed when the Native American captured the post. With the military gone, the area reverted to its position as a commercial center, with a French merchant acting as the British government's representative.

Spain Reigns

No longer used as a military garrison, the fort fell into disrepair. The few who lived there struggled to survive. In 1781, under orders from the Spanish lieutenant governor of St. Louis,

Missouri, a French militia captain along with two chiefs and their men, attacked the fort. The resident traders surrendered without firing a shot. The fort was claimed in the name of Spain, although the Spanish only occupied it for one day. Taking all the fort's stores and provisions, the raiders returned victorious to St. Louis. As soon as the Spanish left town, they lost control of the fort, which lay abandoned.

Possession Is 9/10ths of the Law

A short time later, England and the United States settled their differences in the Treaty of Paris in 1783. Regardless of whether or not England held title to the Fort St. Joseph area, they signed it over to the United States, along with all the territory extending between Lake Michigan and Lake Huron. Fort St. Joseph residents were now Americans.

And the native tribes? Once American settlers moved in, they were forced to cede their homeland. Some tribes made peace with the United States and were relocated to reservations. Others fought to keep their land, but outnumbered and outgunned, most were eventually defeated by American cavalry.

So How Did Fort St. Joe Become Niles?

Although the fort was abandoned after the Spanish conquered it, settlements had already begun to spring up in the area. Near the fort's original site, the village of Niles was platted and recorded in 1829, and named after Hezekiah Niles, a Baltimore newspaper publisher. Thirty years later Niles incorporated as a city. A clever marketer opened the Four Flags Hotel in Niles in 1925, and the area has been known by that moniker ever since.

Go Spartans!

You know you went to Michigan State University if . . .

- You had to walk farther to class than to the local bar.

- You spent more time playing euchre than studying.

- You sat by the Red Cedar and drove on Grand River.

- You know what a Fragel is.

- For two years your smallest class had 500 students in it.

- You spent a night guarding Sparty.

- You still go back for El Azteco.

- You know your sport is basketball.

DID YOU KNOW?

- Thanks to experiments done at MSU (known as "Moo U"), we have homogenized milk.

- The MSU yearbook was called *The Wolverine* from 1900 to 1974. Named after the state animal, it predated rival U of M's mascot choice—the wolverine—by about six months.

Go Wolverines!

You know you went to the University of Michigan if . . .

- You frequent small businesses like the Shaman Drum Bookshop or Espresso Royale.

- You've tailgated in a parking lot, chanting, "State sucks!"

- You drive an SUV, but are pro-environment.

- You thought about running the Naked Mile.

- The word *fishbowl* means long nights in a computer lab.

- Your family won't stop saying how liberal you've become.

- The letters M.L.B. make you shake and yell, "Learning a second language is overrated!"

DID YOU KNOW?

- Madonna attended the University of Michigan for two years on a dance scholarship.

- Composer and conductor John Philip Sousa said that the University of Michigan's fight song, "The Victors," by Louis Elbel, was "the greatest college fight song ever written."

Detroit's Whiskey River

When Prohibition came to Michigan, the people of the
Motor City fueled their Fords with 80-proof whiskey.

In the early 1900s, when it came to combating the evils of demon rum, Michigan citizens were all for law and order. Nearly three years ahead of the 18th amendment, they jumped the gun on nationwide Prohibition by legislating their state "dry" on May 1, 1917, with the Damon Law. At the stroke of the pen in the State House, Michigan's drunkards and tipplers became outlaws. And many other citizens became tourists.

Daytrippers Delight

Nearby Toledo, Ohio, suddenly became a hot spot for Detroiters. So did Windsor and Sault Ste. Marie, Ontario, across the border in Canada. On summer afternoons, boating on the Detroit and St. Clair rivers and picnicking on the Canadian side became more popular than baseball doubleheaders. Young men of Detroit would stroll over the Peace Bridge to Windsor in the morning, and would lumber back in the afternoon—with special harnesses under their coats heavy with quarts of Canadian liquor. Detroit housewives began buying their groceries in Windsor. Matrons embraced Windsor's haute couture, lugging hatboxes from the city's millinery shops back to Detroit almost daily. Young mothers trundled baby carriages to Windsor in even the foulest weather. Detroit's dowagers kept long, full skirts in fashion, though if the women walked too fast, their loot sometimes clinked.

But it wasn't just the pedestrians who were getting the liquor into the state. Almost as fast as Henry's workers were pushing Fords off the assembly line, new car owners were building hiding places for liquor under floorboards and installing additional dummy gas tanks for special, aged, high-proof fuel. Customs agents even nabbed a man who'd filled his car tires with liquor—a blowout that man regretted.

In 1919 Michigan drinkers had a reprieve for a few months when the Damon Law was struck down as unconstitutional. But on January 1, 1920, the federal Volstead Act came into force. Now the entire nation's drinking population faced the Michigan plight. But illicit hooch was already second nature to Michigander drinkers, at least those near the Canadian border.

The Big Business of Booze

Unfortunately for drinkers along the border, there was a problem: the province of Ontario had dried up, too. But Canada's federal government still permitted manufacture of booze for export, which meant that liquor in large quantities could be legally purchased in Canada. Where it went after it left Canada didn't trouble northern officials as long as customs fees were paid and export papers were in order.

On clear mornings, Detroiters could gaze across the Detroit River and see the massive outline of the Hiram Walker distillery at river's edge, knowing that it housed hundreds of thousands of gallons of Canadian Club whiskey. And from the distillery, its owners, brothers Harry and Herbert Hatch, were having a look southward. The brothers had a problem—where to sell their whiskey. It didn't take long for gangsters and the distillers to band together. Soon two private navies appeared on the rivers and lakes. One was Canadian, known as Hatch's Navy, made up mostly of free-enterprising fishing boat owners, and the other was the Little Jewish Navy, which operated from the Detroit waterfront.

On the Canadian side, the deal was simple. A buyer would arrive, fill out customs papers for an export shipment to, say, Cuba, pay the fees, load up, and set sail. Canadian customs people didn't care that the liquor was loaded on a fishing boat that couldn't have made it down Lake Ontario, let alone to Cuba. Nor did they care that the day after its trip to Cuba, it was back for another load. Soon the Detroit River was dotted with customs sheds to handle the traffic.

On the American side, the Little Jewish Navy was not nearly as peaceable as Hatch's crew. Some of its boats were designed (and armed) for hijacking the competition as well. This navy was owned and operated by a group of Jewish Detroit gangsters who had become known as the Purple Gang years before Prohibition gave them a major economic leg up. Their tactics netted them a pretty penny in the liquor-smuggling industry.

In the early 1920s the booze business was booming, in spite of Prohibition. U.S. customs couldn't stem the flow, the Coast Guard didn't have nearly enough ships, and for every gung-ho enforcement agent, seven or eight looked the other way. Plus, most citizens didn't see drinking or the supply of alcohol as a crime. One raid in a Detroit speakeasy netted the mayor, a congressman, and a local sheriff. By 1929 Detroit had 25,000 speakeasies—clandestine quasi-saloons and nightclubs. That year, according to federal government estimates, illicit booze accounted for $215 million dollars of retail revenues in Michigan, second only to the automobile industry. A thousand cases a day crossed the river.

American Ingenuity

As the forces of law and order began to slow the traffic on the water, rum runners submerged themselves. A cable was strung along the river bottom to haul cases of liquor from shore to shore. Then a tunnel was constructed. Supported with stout beams and narrowly tracked like a typical mine tunnel, the liquor was trundled across in mining carts. Nerviest of all was an underwater pipeline direct from a distillery to a bottling plant on the American side.

Fishermen began towing boatloads of booze across the ice with cars and trucks. Sometimes they did it by hand, tortuously dragging their loads on skis, even in blizzards. Worn-out jalopies were pressed into service—if they sank, it wasn't a big deal. Winter car caravans were common, sometimes as many as 75 vehicles in a lurching row. In time all the effort became unnecessary. The "Noble Experiment" of Prohibition ended in 1933. Ironically, Michigan, which had led the way to ban alcohol, was also the first state to cast its vote on the side of the "wets." Prohibition had, in fact, caused alcohol consumption in Michigan and the rest of the country to increase.

Hometown:
Capital City, Lansing

*Though wild and untamed at its inception, Lansing
has grown into a beautiful capital city.*

Town: Lansing
Location: Ingham County
Founding: capital of Michigan, 1847; city, 1859
Current population: 120,000 (est.)
Size: 35 square miles

What's in a Name? One of the area's earliest settlers, Joseph E.
North, petitioned to the legislature for the township to be
named Lansing. North had come from Lansing, New York, and
wanted the new township, built in the untamed wilds of
Michigan, to be named for his hometown.

Claim to Fame:

- In 1847, in a surprising decision by the state legislature, the
  undeveloped township of Lansing won out as the location of
  choice for the new state capital. Until then, the capital had
  been Detroit, but because the town bordered "a foreign

nation," lawmakers decided to move it. Lansing was more secure and centrally located.

- Ransom Olds (inventor of the assembly line and founder of the Olds Motor Vehicle Company, which produced the Oldsmobile) built his first car in Lansing in 1897. His company later became General Motors, which closed in Lansing in 2005 after 99 years of production.

- Until it closed in May 2005, the General Motors Lansing Car Assembly Plant employed some 7,000 workers who turned out more cars than any other plant in the country—approximately 400,000 cars annually, including the Buick Skylark, the Pontiac Grand Am, and the Chevy Malibu. The plant's last car came off the assembly line on May 6, 2005.

- The city is home to Michigan State University (MSU).

- Lansing is also home to a minor league baseball team, the Lansing Lugnuts; the Lansing Cricket Club; and the Lansing Sailing Club.

- The Michigan Library and Historical Center in Lansing boasts the second largest state library in the country, as well as such unique exhibits as facades of a lumber baron's mansion, a walk-through copper mine tunnel, a working sawmill, and a stake fort.

"Strang" but True

Though Beaver Island lists among its past residents the migrating Ottawa tribe, traders, trappers, and fishers, the island is perhaps most famous—or infamous—for having played host to excommunicated Mormon James Jesse Strang.

In 1844, following the death of Mormon Church founder Joseph Smith, James Jesse Strang, a convert to the faith, laid claim to the leadership of the church. Though Strang had his supporters, Brigham Young was the rightful successor as determined by the Mormon Church. Excommunicated by Young, Strang and his followers—known as "Strangites"—set out for Wisconsin, where Strang organized a colony called Voree.

It was in Voree, in 1845, that Strang claimed to have received a heavenly vision, which, among his followers, helped to cement his claims of being a prophet. So when numerous outsiders moved into the area, disrupting the ascetic community he had established, Strang's flock happily followed him to their new home in Beaver Island, Michigan.

I'm King of the World!
Strang and his Strangites landed on Beaver Island in 1848, and it wasn't long before he stirred up trouble again. In 1849, when Strang received another revelation which he claimed sanctioned

polygamy, he began taking multiple wives. In 1850 he crowned himself King James and King of the Kingdom of God on Earth. He attempted to extract tithes not only from his followers, but also from the island's other residents, primarily trappers and fishermen. The Strangites' greater numbers enabled Strang to do so, by force if necessary. He further angered the island's population with his staunch anti-alcohol crusade. Tensions ran high and escalated into fighting and bloodshed when Strang tried to halt the trading of whiskey into the area. Unhappy with Strang's despotism, most of the townspeople fled for the mainland. By 1851 the Strangites had control of nearby Mackinac Island government, which was lumped together with Beaver Island for judicial and elective purposes.

He Fought the Law and the Law Lost

Strang's activities, which became more and more disreputable, didn't go unnoticed. U.S. Congressman Stephen A. Douglas, of neighboring Illinois, brought Strang's activities to the attention of President Millard Fillmore, who eventually intervened and requested that the attorney general prosecute Strang for several federal misdeeds, including delaying mail, evading taxes, and counterfeiting. Strang and many of his followers were brought to Detroit in 1851, in the U.S. Navy steamship *Michigan*, and the trial began. Though all of the defendants were jailed, they were released on Strang's word pending trial. Strang had been a lawyer in the past, which worked in his favor. Against all odds, he won the case and headed home to Beaver Island. This victory only served to heighten his appeal among his followers, and Strang was elected to the state legislature in 1852.

However, Strang's popularity was not to last. His increasingly tyrannical rule alienated his flock. When one of his followers, Thomas Bedford, was caught in the act of adultery and cruelly beaten, he vowed revenge on the king. Bedford enlisted the aid of other disgruntled Strangites and islanders and ambushed Strang. Strang, who received multiple gunshot wounds, headed back to Voree, where he died in his first wife's arms less than a month later. After Strang's death, a group of fishermen and Mackinac Islanders looted and burned the colony, driving most of the Strangites away and reclaiming their land.

Strang's Legacy

The Strangite sect continues today, though they are few in number. If you're in the area, you might want to take a dive in Fox Lake—it is said that Strang dropped some gold there when fleeing Beaver Island. The island now hosts an annual Museum Week—don't forget to stop by the Old Mormon Print Shop Museum, where Strang's doctrines, religious tracts, and newspaper were published. They have several rotating exhibits and one focuses on Strang's time on Beaver Island.

DID YOU KNOW?

In 1914 Henry Ford's book *The Little White Slaver* was published. Written for children shortly after Michigan's 1909 cigarette ban, the book served as an exposé of the known dangers of smoking.

The Best Business Deal in U.S. History, Part I

The early days of the auto industry were like the Internet boom of the 1990s—people could make huge fortunes by investing in the right car company. But no high-tech rags-to-riches story quite matched the return on investment that the Dodge brothers got for their $7,000 in auto parts and $3,000 in cash. It's a great, little-known business tale that we first published in Absolutely Absorbing.

Rags to Roadsters

In 1901, the early days of the automobile, Ransom Eli Olds was looking for subcontractors who could manufacture parts for his Curved Dash Oldsmobile. The best machine shop in the Detroit area was a company called Leland and Faulconer, but they were already committed to supplying parts for the new Cadillac Automobile Company. So Olds turned to the second-best machine shop in town, owned and operated by John and Horace Dodge.

Experience Counts

The brothers Dodge were only in their mid-30s, but they already had more than 20 years' experience working with internal combustion engines. Their father owned a machine shop on the river that connected Lake Huron with Lake Erie, and the brothers spent much of their childhood helping him repair and rebuild ship engines.

By the time John and Horace were in their 20s, both were working as machinists in Detroit. They spent the next several years perfecting their skills at various companies, and in 1897 they opened a bicycle company to manufacture an "improved" bicycle they'd designed themselves. Two years later, they sold the company and used the money—$7,500 in cash and $10,000 worth of machine tools—to open the Dodge Brothers Machine Shop in Detroit.

Shifting Gears

Dodge Brothers started out manufacturing parts for all different types of products, including firearms, bicycles, automobiles, and steam engines. But they got so much business from Olds that they dropped everything else and began manufacturing auto parts exclusively. Olds sold 2,000 cars in 1902, more than any other carmaker in the country, and every one of them had a Dodge transmission. As production continued to climb, Dodge Brothers moved to a newer, larger shop and spent tens of thousands of dollars on new machine tools to keep up with the demand.

Then in 1903 the Dodge brothers took a huge risk: they dumped the Olds Motor Works account and agreed to begin manufacturing engines, transmissions, and chassis for the Ford & Malcomson Company—which, unlike Olds, had only recently opened for business and had yet to manufacture a single car.

Hard Bargain

Why would the Dodge brothers abandon Olds for Ford &
Malcomson? Part of the reason was that Henry Ford, the company's cofounder, had showed them the plans for his Model A
"Fordmobile," and the Dodges were impressed. They thought it
had a good chance of succeeding.

But there was an even bigger incentive: Ironically, Henry
Ford's track record of failure (he had already run two companies into the ground) actually made doing business with him
more lucrative for the Dodge brothers than if he had been a
success. His credit rating was so bad that he had to offer the
brothers a sweeter business deal than they could have found
anywhere else in town.

Normally, in the machine parts industry, an auto company
like Ford & Malcomson would have 60 days to pay for auto
parts after delivery. But because the Dodges weren't sure if Ford
would still be in business in 60 days, they demanded cash up
front on the first shipment of parts, and payment within 15
days on each subsequent delivery. If Ford couldn't pay, ownership of all unsold parts automatically reverted to the Dodge
brothers. The terms were tough, but Ford had to agree.

Howdy, Pardner

There was one more perk. When Henry Ford and Alex
Malcomson, Detroit's leading coal merchant, set out to found
an auto company together, they had hoped to finance the
entire venture with their own savings. But they soon realized
they didn't have enough money: Malcomson's credit was so
overstretched that he took his name off Ford & Malcomson

(renaming it the Ford Motor Company), so his bankers wouldn't find out he had money tied up in the business. (Plus, if the company went under, as Malcomson feared it might, he worried his name would become associated with failure.)

Henry Ford's financial position wasn't much better. He had very little money of his own, and had already alienated Detroit's business community with his two earlier business failures. Nobody wanted to invest in a company run by a two-time loser like Ford.

With so few people willing to invest in Ford, Malcomson pushed the company's stock onto friends and colleagues who owed him favors. He also pitched the shares to people who had a direct financial stake in the company's survival, two of whom were John and Horace Dodge. Malcomson offered them a ten percent stake in the Ford Motor Company, in exchange for $7,000 worth of auto parts and $3,000 in cash.

Turn to page 187 for more of the story.

FORD'S WORDS

"If you have an idea, that's good. If you also have an idea as to how to work it out, that's better."

"Whether you think you can or whether you think you can't, you're right."

"Even a mistake may turn out to be the one thing necessary to a worthwhile achievement."

Off the Beaten Track

Whether you're a Michigander or a tourist, these
wacky roadside attractions are worth a stop.

The World's Largest Tire

Where: Allen Park near Detroit Metro Airport

What: A symbol of a once-booming local industry, this 86-foot tall tire weighs 100 tons and was built to withstand hurricane-force winds.

History: The tire was built as a Ferris wheel by the Uniroyal Tire Company for the 1964 World's Fair in New York. Two million people rode in its 24 gondolas, including Jacqueline Kennedy and the Shah of Iran. When the World's Fair ended, the Ferris wheel was dismantled and the tire was shipped off to Michigan, where it now sits, amusing tourists.

The World's Largest Hairball

Where: Anthony Hall, Michigan State University, East Lansing

What: It is indeed the world's largest hairball.

History: The pride of the Michigan State Agriculture Department, the hairball was discovered in the stomach of a cow—it's the size of a basketball. Unlike cats, it seems cows cannot cough up hairballs.

Da Yoopers Tourist Trap & Museum

Where: Ishpeming, on Highway 41, about 15 miles west of Marquette

What: Wonderfully cheesy tourist stuff—and the world's largest working chain saw. In the gift shop, you can buy original artwork from local artists, as well as such offerings as canned fresh air, canned partridge gonads, and fish bottoms.

History: Da Yoopers is the name of a local comedy band, whose leader, Jim "Hoolie" DeCaire, is also the proprietor of Da Yoopers Tourist Trap & Museum. The band pokes gentle fun at the culture, customs, and rural ways of area residents. And that's pretty much the museum's mission as well. Much of the humor is crass, coarse, and hilarious. The most famous "exhibit"—and our personal favorite—is the two-seater, Da Yoopers' outhouse (the holes are one above the other), titled "The Reading Room."

Michigan's Largest Cherry Pie Pan

Where: Traverse City

What: The pan in which the world's then-largest cherry pie was baked.

History: A record-breaking cherry pie (17 feet 6 inches in diameter and 28,350 pounds) was unveiled on July 25, 1987 (a year that saw a bumper crop of sour cherries), at the annual Traverse City Cherry Festival. To cook the massive dessert, the gas company ran a line to a specially built concrete oven. Traverse City retained the record until 1992, when a small town in British Columbia broke the record for the largest cherry pie.

We Got Game

In 1966 two of the greatest college teams of all time—Michigan State University and Notre Dame—duked it out for the national collegiate championship. In the pre-Super Bowl era, this was the game to catch. And this game would change the sport of football.

In 1966 the Notre Dame Fighting Irish was the number-one ranked football team in the country, and the Michigan State University Spartans was number two. Rankings were bestowed by polls of sportswriters and coaches and, thus, hotly debated.

Spartan Social Justice

In 1966 Spartan fans were in their glory. Michigan State University's coach, Duffy Daugherty, had assembled a history-making football team—a winning team that had broken the color barrier. The 1964 Civil Rights Act had made discrimination illegal, but two years later no African American collegiates played below the Mason Dixon line. And those who played on northern teams weren't deemed capable of playing key positions like quarterback. Duffy Daugherty changed all that. Caring only about ability, he raided the South for rejected African American athletes. Michigan's integrated team had two African American captains, Clinton Jones on offense and George Webster on defense. Helping the Spartans create the best defensive team in MSU's history were African American captains Charlie "Bubba Smith" and Charlie "Mad Dog" Thornhill. On offense was black quarterback Jimmy Raye. The Spartans were out to prove that integrated teams with African Americans in key leadership positions could win, and win big. In 1966 they were winning every game. In November they were pitted against the Fighting Irish.

Fighting Irish Glory

Notre Dame's coach Ara Parseghian did not have to search for talent. Nearly every aspiring high school football star wanted to play for the Fighting Irish. Since 1924, when they had won their first national championship, they'd become the nation's best-known college football team.

Despite their fame, for several previous years their team had been mediocre at best. But that all changed in 1966. Throughout their season, Notre Dame, like MSU, remained undefeated. In addition, Notre Dame shut out five teams and beat their opponents by an average of 34 points. Hailed as the players who had helped restore their school to gridiron glory, quarterback Terry Hanratty (with a record-shattering passing arm) and his receiver, Jim Seymour, had already made the cover of *Time* magazine.

Showdown in East Lansing

People grumbled that Notre Dame had always been the darling of sportswriters, and that Michigan had been robbed. Whatever the polls said, fans, sportswriters, players, and coaches believed that the upcoming matchup would decide the true champion. Pregame excitement was so high that some colleges canceled their football games due to worries that fans would not attend, choosing instead to stay home and watch the big game on TV.

On game day, in Spartan Stadium, more than 76,000 fans cheered their lungs out as the teams took their positions. Notre Dame player Rocky Bleier called the situation, "clearly, the edge of insanity." The game's beginning was disastrous for Notre Dame. Their star running back couldn't play—he'd hurt himself off the field, slipping in icy Michigan weather. Worse, in the first quarter, Terry Hanratty was steamrolled by the huge Bubba Smith and left the game with a separated shoulder.

Michigan took advantage of Notre Dame's plight to score a touchdown. They continued to dominate the first half, and Dick Kenny made one of his famous barefoot kicks to score a field goal and raise their lead to ten points. But Notre Dame came back just before the half with a touchdown.

The Fourth Downer

In the fourth quarter, after Notre Dame scored a field goal, the teams were tied at 10–10. The fans went wild! The game went into its final moments. But it all ended in a tie. What?

Notre Dame's coach decided not to pass or call time-out for the last six downs. Parseghian made his team keep the ball and let the clock run out, figuring a tie was better than a loss. If Notre Dame was defeated and Michigan remained undefeated, Notre Dame might not be able to retain its number-one ranking and the national championship.

Notre Dame went on to beat its next opponent, USC, 51–0. They were considered undefeated, declared the best team, and became the national champions. Parseghian was

proved right, but angry fans and sportswriters disliked his calculated decision. The day that had begun with such excitement
ended in frustration, and the game of the century became "that
@#&^% tie game." And a lot of the expletives were reserved
for Parseghian. Some fans and sportswriters demanded that tie
games should go into overtime like baseball until a winner was
declared, but the rules remained the same. Few coaches have
since made the decision that brought Parseghian so much flak.

Channeling Changes

For all the disappointment surrounding it, the big game did
bring big changes to college football. The networks had televised college games before, but they'd never seen interest or
viewership like this. The millions of fans that tuned in made
school administrators aware of how powerful—not to mention
lucrative—the combination of college sports and television
could be. TV and college football were wedded from that day
forward. Previously school administrations had barred bowl
game champions from returning the next year, giving more
schools a chance to play a bowl game. That practice changed,
so that now only the top winning teams played in bowl games,
regardless of how many times they had played before. Playing
schedules were also changed so that top teams would play each
other at the end of the season to battle for bowl games. All of
this was aimed at keeping interest—and TV ratings—high.
And, most importantly, schools realized that fans cared about
great football and not about the color of the players, which
helped bring an end to the practice of keeping African
Americans off Southern teams and out of key positions.

Through the Mill

Here's a look at Jiffy's sweet road to success.

A gargantuan 23 x 50-foot blue-and-white box of corn muffin mix looms over downtown Chelsea, Michigan, home of the Chelsea Milling Company, which produces an icon of home cooking—Jiffy mixes. The real success of the 118-year-old company, which started with the family flour mill business in 1887, is tied up in the apron strings of Mabel White Holmes, the mill owner's wife, and grandmother of Howdy Holmes, the firm's current president and CEO.

Filling a Knead

In 1930 Howdy's dad, Howard, and Howard's twin brother, Dudley, invited two friends over. The young visitors, raised by their single-parent father, brought their own lunch. Mrs. Holmes peeked into their bags and saw biscuits—not soft, fluffy biscuits, but "something that looked more like a hockey puck." Inspired by the father's attempt at baking, Mabel embarked on a mission to produce "a mix that is so easy, even a man could do it." Her husband knew it was a product that both men and housewives could appreciate and supported her mission to create the first prepared baking mix. Mabel spent countless hours perfecting the recipe and determining exactly how many servings a box should contain—one that would make just enough for one family's dinner.

Ready in a Jiffy!

Mabel needed a short, catchy name for her quick and easy product. She recalled a family cook who would request, "Now, Miss Mabel, you tell your father them good hot biscuits will be ready in a jiffy!" So Jiffy it was. The first major customer was C.F. Smith stores in Detroit, and Jiffy got a big boost when Dr. Royal S. Copeland, former mayor of Ann Arbor and future health commissioner of New York City, tested the mix and raved about it in his syndicated newspaper column.

It was smooth milling until 1936, when Mabel's husband fell off a factory lift while checking the temperature inside the silo. After the tragedy, Mabel became company president, and her sons assisted. Howard oversaw sales and administration, and Dudley supervised the flour mill and procurement. Additional mixes were added along the way, including piecrust in 1940 and corn muffin mix in 1950. Less popular products, such as doughnut mix, got shelved along the way. Mabel retired in 1944, and Howard took the helm as president, with Dudley as vice president.

From 1930 to the early 1960s, the firm played a dual role, selling both commercial-brand flour and Jiffy mixes. But, in the early 1960s, the demand for Jiffy mixes had risen so much, that all of the commercial flour was needed for the mix division. Chelsea Milling still retains its distinction as a flour miller today, but all of the flour is now used for Jiffy.

Topping the Charts

Jiffy mixes are pretty much no-nonsense products. The company doesn't advertise or issue coupons, but instead relies on word of mouth. "We have the price point advantage," Howdy boasts. While the mixes sell for as low as 35 cents each, the firm continues to rake in the dough, accounting for 58 percent of the nation's overall market for baking mix products and 65 percent of the value—or low cost—market.

The company started so many years ago—which now includes more family members and about 350 employees—is more complicated now and the tempo is faster. Still, no part of the process is outsourced, and, after all these years, Chelsea Milling Company still tops the muffin mix hit parade. "That," says Howdy, "is as good as it gets."

DID YOU KNOW?

- The fruit in the Jiffy muffin mixes are dried apples bathed in blueberry and raspberry flavoring. Apples dry well and simulate the taste and texture of the other fruits very nicely. "We're not being sneaky. It's on the box, and we've done a good job," says Howdy.

- Corn muffin mix is the most popular mix, followed by blueberry muffin mix.

- Approximately 1.6 million boxes are produced daily.

- Jiffy produces 18 different types of mixes.

A Model Puzzle

Here are 35 car models wheeling and dealing through one of Henry Ford's finest, a Model A.

ALERO	FORD
ASTRO	GEO
AVEO	GMC
AZTEK	GRAND AM
BONNEVILLE	GTO
BUICK	HUMMER
CADILLAC	ION
CAVALIER	LA CROSSE
CENTURY	LE SABRE
CHEVROLET	MALIBU
CONCORDE	MONTANA
CORVETTE	NEON
DE VILLE	REGAL
ENVOY	TAHOE
ESCALADE	VIBE
ESCAPE	VUE
EXPLORER	YUKON
FOCUS	

For answers, turn to page 302.

```
                  R M G H F V R O L E T E
                  B K C I U B O X V E D
                  L O B R A N P P W O A
                  N E N C D L F O T X L
                  Q E O N O S E G M C A
          P Z G F E O H A T W O K Y R E G A L A B C
    R M Y U K O N U X B N H Q E L U V X D R V S D E
    C E U B E E S M A D N A R G I V W I O N K E R D L       C
      Y I I T L V M O N T A N A Z R L M L W I S O R A S T
      E Q L Z L W E M E R B A S E L A Z B L T C F O C U S
    R   K A A I N R L S O R T S A L E R O I E A I C R       F
      A M   V   Y R U T N E C O R V E T T E P C N O
      B W O E A                             L E D O S M
        Y II D O O                          A P G S N
          S C L                             G W E
```

For Love of the Game

Dim the lights and let's get started with this
Michigan sports film festival.

Somewhere in Georgia (1917)

Based on a story by famed baseball writer Grantland Rice, in
this 30-minute silent-era flick, Ty Cobb plays a fictional version of himself returning home to Georgia for an exhibition
game, when a nasty banker has him kidnapped. Luckily Cobb
didn't mind playing rough; in no time at all he whips the bad
guys, gets the girl, and makes it to the game on time.

Harmon of Michigan (1941)

Michigan Wolverine football legend and Heisman Trophy winner Tom Harmon plays a fictional version of himself in this
film, in which he goes from recent college grad to head football
coach during the course of a season (or so it seems; the film's
timeline is a little fuzzy). Its appeal is limited mostly to folks
who can't get enough of "Ole 98." Harmon went on to establish
himself as a top-flight sports announcer for many years before
his death in 1990.

Paper Lion (1968)

Could writer George Plimpton hack it as a player with the Detroit Lions? He tried once, for a story he was writing. This film is based on Plimpton's experience with the Lions and substitutes a pre-*M*A*S*H* Alan Alda for the actual Plimpton. The film uses a number of actual football players of the time for realism, among them Alex Karras and Frank Gifford, and also features a performance by Vince Lombardi. Anyone who likes football films and seeing snobs viciously manhandled on the gridiron will no doubt get a kick out of these proceedings.

The Life and Times of Hank Greenberg (1998)

The first major Jewish player in baseball in Detroit, Hank Greenberg stepped up to the plate and whacked the ball out of the park, helping guide the Tigers to four pennants and two World Series victories in the 1930s, all while maintaining his faith. This engrossing documentary blends archival interview footage of Greenberg with contemporary footage of notable admirers, ranging from Alan Dershowitz to Walter Matthau, who reveal how important a role model he was to the Jewish people.

For Love of the Game (1999)

Kevin Costner plays a Detroit Tigers pitcher at the end of his career who reminisces on the last five years of his life, contemplates the wreck of a relationship he's having with costar Kelly Preston, and tries to pitch a perfect game. Unlike most major motion pictures, this one doesn't have the happiest of endings.

Godfather of the U.P.

As far as we know, Dominic Jacobetti never broke any kneecaps or sent anyone to sleep with the fishes, but the 21-term congressman must have made voters an offer they couldn't refuse: how else to explain his tenure as the longest-serving legislator in Michigan history?

The son of Italian immigrants, Dominic Jacobetti grew up in Negaunee, Michigan. Like his father, he worked in the Athens iron mine, joining the mine workers' ranks in 1940. In 1942 he married Marie Burnette, and they had three children. True to his motto—*siempri avanti,* or "always forward"—he quickly rose through the ranks, going on to become president of United Steelworkers Local 2867, and later, USW Local 4950. This experience would serve him well in his unmatched 40-year career as a Michigan legislator.

A Yooper Through and Through

Elected to the Michigan House of Representatives in 1954, Jacobetti was a Yooper advocate from the outset. Representing at different times the 108th, 109th, and 110th Districts, he spearheaded the campaign to locate the state's second veteran's facility in the Upper Peninsula. And as head of the Michigan

House Appropriations Committee, he was always looking for ways to steer more money to the U.P. for improving its residents' lives, noting, "It's not the monetary values in life that concern me, it's the human values."

Speaking of appropriations, Jacobetti knew a good slogan when he saw one. In 1982 Michigan launched a "Say Yes to Michigan" tourism campaign, prompting one Marquette resident to create "Say Yah to Da U.P., Eh!" bumper stickers. Jacobetti generated his own stickers: "Say Yah to Da U.P. and Jacobetti Too."

Da U.P.: The 51st State

Though Jacobetti worked tirelessly to bring economic opportunities to the U.P. and pushed through seat belt legislation, insurance reform, and tax limitations, the secret to his longevity may have been his attempt to bestow statehood upon the region. In 1978 he introduced a bill that would have created the State of Superior, encompassing the U.P. and a few lower peninsula islands. Surprisingly, the bill never came to a vote, but for many residents of the U.P., the dream and Jacobetti's legacy are still alive. Secessionists occasionally still take up the State of Superior battle cry, inspired largely by their view that the state's politicians shape their policies based primarily on lower peninsula concerns. Even if these folks are serious, though, the U.P.'s dependence on tax dollars and other state funds suggest that we shouldn't expect a 51st state anytime soon.

Jacobetti died on November 28, 1994, just a few weeks into his 21st term. He is buried in his birthplace.

A Bowler's Paradise

Famous for its breweries, it's no surprise that Michigan is the "kingpin" of a sport historically associated with beer—bowling!

European immigrants brought various forms of bowling to America in the 1800s, but today's sport most resembles ninepin, which was introduced to the colonies by Dutch settlers. In 1842 the tenth pin was added, and German immigrants helped to popularize the game, which was commonly played in saloons. Bowling boomed during the early 20th century, and by the 1950s Detroit had the biggest sponsors (mostly breweries) and was known as the city where good bowlers came and found fame. Michigan tops the list for the most sanctioned bowlers (competing in accordance with American Bowling Congress or Women's International Bowling Congress rules) in the United States, so many of our future bowling stars will undoubtedly hail from the "kingpin state."

Bowling for Glory

Michigan has had its share of record-holding teams and bowlers:

- Stroh's Bohemian Beer, Detroit: ABC National Tournament team title (1934)

- E & B Beer, Detroit: ABC National Tournament team title (1952)

- Pfeiffer Beer, Detroit: ABC National Tournament team champions (1953, 1955, 1959)

- Detroit's Joe Norris, one of Michigan's preeminent bowlers, holds the American Bowling Congress (ABC) total pinfall record of 123,770 for 642 games over a 70-year period.

- Marion Ladewig, a native of Grand Rapids, earned Women's International Bowling Congress (WIBC) all-events titles in 1950 and 1955 and was inducted into the WIBC Hall of Fame in 1964.

- Detroit's Aleta Sill was the first woman to reach the $1 million mark in earnings on the Professional Women's Bowling Association tour.

Hitting the Lanes

Here are some of the more unique bowling alleys to check out if you're in the neighborhood:

- **Oldest:** The Garden Bowl in Detroit, built in 1913, has 16 lanes and is the oldest active bowling center in the United States. "Rock 'N' Bowl," which features glow-in-the-dark bowling and live DJs is a popular activity.

- **Largest:** Allen Park's Thunderbowl Lanes is Michigan's largest facility with 94 lanes. It's also the home of the Greater Detroit Bowling Hall of Fame.

- **Smallest:** There are several four-lane centers in Michigan, but the Grand Rapids Home for Veterans has a two-lane bowling alley in the basement for its appreciative members.

- **Most Unusual:** The Clique Bowling Center in Grand Rapids is a double-decker alley with 16 lanes on two floors. Known as "the Clique" to locals, it's a favorite neighborhood hangout, with a classic neon sign of a bowling ball and pin, advertising "bowling, liquor, and beer."

BASIC BOWLING TIPS

1. Be consistent, focus, and concentrate on your target.

2. Relax before every shot. Wipe the oil off your bowling ball with a towel, set up, and take a deep breath or two before you begin your approach.

3. Practice, practice, practice! Bowl at your own pace and work on your spare game during practice. Strikes are wonderful, but if you want to graduate from being a good bowler to a great one, consistently making spares is the key.

4. Maintain a positive attitude, particularly when you make a bad shot or shoot a low score. Shake it off and think positively about the next frame or game.

5. Have fun! Never, ever use your bowling towel as a crying towel.

The Resort That Segregation Built

For more than 50 years, Idlewild, a small town 60 miles north of Grand Rapids and 180 miles northwest of Detroit, gave city-weary African Americans a summer vacation spot to call their own.

Beginning in 1912 and lasting through the 1960s, Idlewild was the largest and most famous playground for African American intellectuals, entertainers, and families. Ironically, it was the brainchild of a wealthy group of white Chicago developers, who purchased 2,700 acres of timberland on the edge of Manistee National Forest and established small lots, which they sold to influential African Americans like sociologist W. E. B. DuBois.

At the time African Americans were not permitted in public places like hotels and restaurants. So Idlewild was an idyllic respite from everyday life, where they could lounge by the lake, camp, ride horses, stroll forested lanes, and never once see a sign that said "Whites Only."

Jump, Jive, and Wail

Idlewild's natural beauty was a backdrop to the best in entertainment, drawing performers from across the nation to its stages. The list was impressive: Louis Armstrong, Sarah Vaughn, Duke

Ellington, Count Basie, Etta James, Jackie Wilson, the Four Tops, Stevie Wonder, and even a young comedian named Bill Cosby. The streets filled with celebrities like Joe Louis, Langston Hughes, and writer Zora Neale Hurston.

Hot Fun in the Summertime!

By the 1950s the place was really hopping, with 15 motels, nine nightclubs, and six restaurants. Its name has no official history, but some old-timers say it stood for the "idle men and wild women" who gave Idlewild its joie de vivre.

The most famous hotels were the Flamingo, the Paradise, and El Morocco, where Sammy Davis Jr. danced his heart out. "The music and the applause tended to soothe a lot of problems related to segregation. We couldn't stay in the finest hotels, and certain restaurants didn't want to serve you," crooner Jerry "the Iceman" Butler once told the *Washington Post*. "But Idlewild secluded you from all that."

The Party's Over . . . Or Is It Just Beginning?

With the end of segregation came the end of Idlewild. Its former patrons now had the freedom to vacation wherever they chose, and performers and vacationers headed to resorts in hot spots like Las Vegas and Florida. The city became a ghost town, home to only 400 people, a few motels, and four churches.

There have been some recent attempts to revive the community, including the annual Idlewild Jazz Festival, which is held every August. Those interested in experiencing a bit of history can also visit the recreated Idlewild Clubhouse, a living history exhibit, at Greenfield Village in Dearborn.

Making the Best of a Cold Situation

Citizens in other states may huddle inside during winter's frigid months, but Michiganders turn the blistering cold into a reason to party. Whether they're holding a fishing pole over a hole in the ice or building a snow castle as big as a house, they have a talent for finding ways to freeze.

Red Flannel Festival

Where: Cedar Springs

When: Early October

In 1936, while much of the country was overwhelmed by record snowfall and subzero temperatures, a New York writer complained that, "Here we are in the midst of an old-fashioned winter and there are no red flannels in the USA to go with it." Nina Babcock and Grace Hamilton, of Michigan's *Cedar Springs Clipper,* answered with an editorial that said, "Just because Saks Fifth Avenue does not carry red flannels, it does not follow that no one in the country does. CEDAR SPRINGS' merchants have red flannels!" The Associated Press picked up the story and, as a result of all the attention, Cedar Springs created Red Flannel Day to celebrate their lumbering history and famous "drop seaters," as the flannels with flaps around the rear are called. More than six decades later, it's still celebrated with the Lumberjack Supper, old-time entertainment, crafts, and a parade.

Mancelona Buck Pole
Where: Mancelona
When: Mid-November
The Mancelona Chamber of Commerce annually hosts northern Michigan's oldest and most beloved Buck Pole. On the first weekend of deer hunting season, a two-day party is thrown to commemorate the returning hunters' successes. Prizes are awarded to the hunters who bring down the heaviest deer, the deer with the widest rack spread, and the deer with the most points on its rack, as well as for the first hunter to return from the surrounding woods with a deer to hang from the massive buck pole. Nowhere in Michigan can hunters find a better opportunity to exchange stories and photos of their hunts, tell tall tales of the buck that got away, and stuff themselves with venison.

Michigan Tech Winter Carnival
Where: Houghton
When: Early February
Houghton during the winter is what writers must have envisioned when they coined the term "Great White North." To commemorate the incredible amount of snow that blankets the town every year, Michigan Technological University throws a five-day winter carnival that draws visitors from all over the state. College students host the biggest attraction, the all-night snow statue sculpting contest, where garage-sized feats of icy

engineering are produced. For everyone else, there's a sled-dog race, ice bowling, broomball, snowboarding, cross-country skiing, ice fishing, snow volleyball, stage reviews, and curling. A Winter Carnival queen is crowned, and fireworks wow the crowds.

North American Snowmobile Festival
Where: Cadillac
When: Early February
Situated at the heart of the Northern Michigan Snow Belt, Cadillac has become the hub of an outstanding snowmobile trail system that offers easy cross-state connections. Essentially, it is the mecca of Michigan snowmobilers, which is why it hosts the four-day North American Snowmobile Festival, attracting some 10,000 sleds every year. Here you can test your machine against the gun in the Radar Run or go one-on-one against your buddies in a Grudge Drag. Other activities include the frigid but popular Polar Dip, a snow sculpture competition, an ice-fishing contest, the Great American Chili Cook-Off (hosted by WTCM radio, the cook-off usually draws about 2,500 chili buffs), and the AMA Motorcycle Races (the multi-class oval track racing even takes place on the ice).

Hometown:
Middle of the Mitten

Town: Midland
Location: Midland County
Founding: 1856; incorporated 1897
Current population: 42,000 (est.)
Size: approximately 33 square miles

What's in a Name? Midland bears the same name as the county in which it resides, and was given its name because it is in the middle of the state. Its nickname, "Dow town," comes from Herbert H. Dow, the inventor/humanitarian who revitalized the struggling logging town with a new chemical industry in the 1890s.

Claim to Fame:

- Midland is one of three towns (Saginaw and Bay City form the rest of the triumvirate) that make up the "tri-cities" in the state.

- The city's economy largely depends on the production of chemicals extracted from the brine (a salt solution) found in deep natural wells under the flatlands. The chemicals are used to produce pharmaceutical, agricultural, and petro-chemical products worldwide. Two Fortune 500 companies that have resulted from the industry, Dow Chemical and Dow Corning, are based in Midland and employ thousands of people.

- In the heart of downtown is the Tridge, a three-way foot-bridge built in 1981 that spans the confluence of the Tittabawassee and Chippewa rivers. It is a popular local recreational area with parks and trails on every side.

- Chemicals aren't the only things the town produces. Cathy Guisewite, who writes the nationally syndicated *Cathy* comic strip, graduated from Midland High in 1968. Dr. Earl L. Warrick, inventor of Silly Putty, also hails from Midland.

PUPPY RECORDS

Brandy, a fawn-colored boxer, became a star in St. Clair Shores after making an appearance on the "Ripley's Believe It or Not" television show because of her astounding 17-inch tongue. One of her favorite tricks is eating from a bowl placed 13 inches away from her mouth. Brandy's family purchased the dog from a breeder back in 1995 who said that she would "grow into her tongue."

Buddy, a cocker spaniel from Muskegon County, has what may be the world's longest dog eyelashes. He beat the previous record by a full inch with lashes that measure an astounding 4.7 inches!

Shipwreck!

*Paradise, Michigan, off Whitefish Bay, is the diving
capital—and the ship graveyard—of the Great Lakes.*

Paradise, Michigan, at the northeastern tip of Michigan's
Upper Peninsula, is famous for its forests, waterfalls, and
vast beaches. But one of its most intriguing attractions lies
deep within Lake Superior—the 376-square-mile Whitefish
Point Underwater Preserve.

Shipwreck Coast

Shipping on the Great Lakes took off after 1847 when copper
and iron ore were discovered along Lake Superior's shores.
Since then billions of tons of cargo have crossed through the
Great Lakes St. Lawrence Seaway System, which connects the
Great Lakes with the Atlantic Ocean. But not all ships have
made the trip successfully. From sailing schooners of the 1800s
to modern bulk freighters, or "lakers," over 6,000 ships have
sunk in Great Lakes waters.

Lake Superior's 160 miles of open water make it the world's
largest body of inland water. It is also the most treacherous of
the Great Lakes, and its most deadly stretch lies off of
Whitefish Point, a rock outcropping jutting out of the middle

of Whitefish Bay. The bay sits on the eastern end of Lake Superior where shipping traffic is heavy. Lakers departing from myriad harbors all have to pass this way to enter St. Marys River and the Soo Canal. At the same time, they have to avoid oncoming traffic. Bad weather intensifies the congestion, and the bay is notorious for thick fog and snow squalls that limit visibility—with disastrous results. Most of the nor'easters originate in the Canadian northwest, and by the time they arrive at Whitefish Point, they can reach hurricane force. Traveling over the vast open water, the winds can whip up 30-foot waves. The bay is also on the eastern end of an 80-mile-long, low, rugged shoreline that traps ships on sandbars—a shoreline so deadly it has been called Superior's shipwreck coast. Vessels caught in high seas near the bay have no safe harbor.

The Wreck of the *Edmund Fitzgerald*

More vessels have been lost at Whitefish Point than in any other part of the Great Lakes. The most famous is the *Edmund Fitzgerald*, which sunk on November 10, 1975, a loss that put fear into everyone who worked on lakers. Built in Michigan, the *Edmund Fitzgerald* was 729 feet long and weighed 13,632 tons and was one of the largest lakers of her day, well built, and graciously appointed. The great ship was on her way to Detroit when she broke apart and went down 17 miles from Whitefish Point. No one knows the exact cause, but Superior's triple hoodoo of snow, gales, and huge waves were all in force.

The *Samuel Mather*, 246 feet long and weighing 1,576 gross tons was a late 19th-century wooden propeller steamer designed to carry bulk freight. In thick fog, the *Mather* collided with another freighter and sunk. Over a century later, in 2004, the Great Lakes Shipwreck Historical Society sent a team to explore the *Mather*. Her superstructure and second mast, complete with rigging, were intact. The cold waters keep sunken ships well preserved. For scholars seeking to learn more about marine history, shipwrecks like the *Mather* are treasures.

Diving in Paradise

Shipwreck divers flock to Paradise not only because of the well-preserved wrecks, but also because the clear waters make it easy to explore sunken vessels. Shipwreck hunters come, too, hoping to be the first to discover a "ghost ship" like the schooner *Frank Perew*. It sunk in heavy seas in 1891 and is believed to rest somewhere off the point.

Whitefish Bay has so many historic wrecks and so much activity underwater that in the 1980s, the state created a marine park. The Whitefish Point Underwater Preserve protects shipwrecks from being stripped and preserves them for study and exploration.

While divers hit the depths of the marine park, landlubbers can tour the Great Lakes Shipwreck Museum at Whitefish Bay. The museum provides an above-water exploration of the sunken ships lying offshore. Artifacts from famous wrecks are displayed, including a 200-pound bronze bell recovered from the *Fitzgerald*. The bell is a memorial to the 29-member crew who rest in the lake.

Birth of a Giant, Part II

They never tell you things like this in school, but the father of the modern bathtub—a real bathroom hero—was also the father of General Motors. Or at least the grandfather. Here's Part II of the story. (Part I starts on page 9.)

In 1904 William Crapo Durant became the head of the Buick Motor Company. Durant was so well known as a successful businessman that when he began his first official task, selling stock in Buick to the public, he found no shortage of takers. In a few short months, he had raised Buick's capital from $75,000 to more than $1.5 million.

Next, Durant set to work designing cars, setting up a network of Buick dealers, and building what was then the largest automobile factory in the United States. The company grew by leaps and bounds: in 1904 Buick had sold fewer than 30 cars in its entire history. By the end of 1906 it had sold more than 2,000 cars, was building 250 new ones a week, and couldn't keep up with the orders that poured in.

Come Together

In 1907 a financial panic rocked Wall Street, and although Buick emerged from the crisis even stronger than it had been before, Durant was convinced that the best way to weather future hard times was for the "Big Four" auto companies—Buick, Ford, REO (founded by Ransom E. Olds after he was forced out of the Olds Motor Works), and Maxwell-Briscoe (cofounded by the Briscoe brothers with the money they made selling their Buick stock)—to merge into one large company. In Durant's vision, each company would swap its own stock for shares in the new company.

According to *A Most Unique Machine*'s author, George S. May, the scheme might have worked except that Henry Ford wanted $3 million in cash. Not to be outdone by Ford, Olds changed his mind and also insisted on $3 million in cash. Durant didn't have $6 million in cash, so the deal quickly collapsed. On September 1, 1908, Durant created his own new company and called it General Motors.

Boom and Bust

Two months after he founded General Motors, Durant bought the Olds Motor Works. The company had fallen on hard times since Ransom Olds had left to found REO, and as Durant soon learned, there weren't even any plans in the works for new Oldsmobiles. "We just paid a million dollars for road signs," he complained to an assistant.

A few days later Durant came up with an idea for a quick fix. He showed up at the Olds plant with a new Buick and asked workers to saw the car's chassis into quarters. He moved the left and right sides of the car six inches apart and lengthened it by a foot.

"Make your new car a little longer, a bit wider, and with more leg room than my Buick," he told the workers. "It will look like an Oldsmobile when you put your radiator and hood on it. And there, with paint and upholstery, is next year's Oldsmobile." The new car, priced at $250 more than the Buick, sold so well that the Olds division was making a profit by the end of the year.

Two months later Durant bought the Oakland Motor Car Company, the predecessor to GM's Pontiac division; six months after that, he bought Cadillac, then one of the most profitable auto manufacturers in the country. In the meantime, he also snapped up a number of companies that supplied GM with auto parts.

Bye-Bye, Billy

If Durant had stopped there, GM might have remained healthy. But he didn't. "Instead of consolidating his gains around the great Buick and Cadillac potential, and their suppliers such as Weston-Mott and AC Sparkplug," Richard Crabb writes in *Birth of a Giant,* "Durant brought into General Motors a long list of firms that held patents on devices which he thought might provide important improvements for the future . . . He chased patents as some boys chase butterflies."

By the end of 1909 Durant had acquired 13 different auto companies and 10 auto parts companies, most of which were money losers that drained profits from his healthy divisions. Things came to a head in 1910, when sales at Buick and Cadillac slumped to the point where Durant didn't have enough cash to make his payroll and pay his bills.

Durant figured he would need about $7 million to weather the crisis, but he wasn't sure—he had acquired companies so fast and kept so many of the details in his head that GM's financial records were several weeks behind. By the time the records were sorted out, it turned out that Durant actually needed more than $12 million to meet his obligations.

Durant's bankers were aghast at the mess he had made of GM, but the company had grown so big so fast that they could hardly afford to let it fail: if GM crashed, it might take the entire Detroit economy with it. So they lent GM the money it needed . . . on the condition that Durant turn over control of GM to the bankers themselves, who would oversee the running of the company until the loans were repaid. There was no other way out, so on November 15, 1910, Durant announced his retirement.

For Part III of the GM story, turn to page 177.

DID YOU KNOW?

Michigan's state slogan on its license plate is "Water Wonderland." Michigan has 11,000 inland lakes. The slogan "Land of 10,000 Lakes" belongs to Minnesota, which has 15,000 inland lakes.

The four interstates that enter Michigan also end there:
I-69 from Indianapolis, Indiana, ends in Port Huron.
I-75 from Fort Meyers, Florida, ends in Sault Ste. Marie.
I-94 from Billings, Montana, ends in Port Huron.
I-96 from Muskegon, Michigan, ends at Detroit's Ambassador Bridge.

Pop Goes Detroit

For nearly a century, Faygo pop has been manufactured in Detroit, for which we can thank two bakers from Russia.

More than half the soft drinks sold in Michigan are not cola drinks but flavored soft drinks instead. Michigan's penchant for these drinks goes back over 95 years when Russian bakers Ben and Perry Feigenson decided to try their luck at making and selling soda in Detroit. The brothers peddled their drinks from a horse-drawn wagon. Detroiters who put down three cents for a bottle of soda found the flavors unlike any other drink they had ever tasted. That was because the brothers made their original flavors—grape, fruit punch, and strawberry—based on their Russian frosting recipes.

Eventually their pop was so successful that they opened the Feigenson Brothers Bottling Works in 1907, which grew into a multimillion dollar company. Decades later Detroiters are still slaking their thirst with Ben and Perry's soft drinks, though the name was changed to Faygo—the shorter name was easier to put on the bottles.

Rock and Rye!
Faygo was referred to as "pop," for the noise the bottle made

when it was opened. Even today—thanks to Faygo—folks in Michigan and many parts of the Midwest will ask for pop when they want a soft drink.

From 1935 on, Faygo pop was produced at the Detroit plant at 3579 Gratiot Street. Unique flavors like Lithiated Lemon became brand hallmarks. The flavor Rock & Rye, a shot of rye whiskey with an ice cube, was a huge success, while the wine-flavored Chateaux Faygeaux was a flop. Regardless, sales continued to grow. By the time Feigensons' sons joined the management team in 1946, Faygo was a Michigan institution and was soon selling in 32 states.

Snack Break

Faygo hit it big with their commercial starring the "Faygo kid" in the 1950s. The animated ad showed Black Bart trying to rob the Wells Faygo stagecoach until the Faygo kid saved the day—and the root beer. The slogan, "Which way did he go? Which way did he go? He went for Faygo!" became a phenomenon, and the winning ad further boosted sales of the pop.

Michigan baby boomers in the 1960s loved the tasty combo of Faygo Redpop (strawberry flavor) and Better Made Potato Chips (also produced on Gratiot Street). The combo remains a favorite, and Faygo now also has a line of diet pops.

Faygo was sold to the National Beverage Corporation in 1987 and it accounts for about 25 percent of the company's sales. New flavors are still added or tossed. In the 1990s a Cherry Festival flavor (made with Michigan cherries) was introduced to honor the Traverse City festival. In 1996 noncarbonated drinks were also added. Anyone up for some Ohana Mango Tango?

Odd Michigan Laws

*Be careful what you do—and where you do it. You
just might find yourself on the wrong side of the law.*

Don't Do It in Detroit

Here's some of what the Motor City has made illegal:

- Husbands can't scowl at their wives on Sunday.

- You can't let your pig run free without a ring in its nose.

- Ogling a woman from a moving car is prohibited.

- Couples are forbidden from making whoopee in their cars,
  unless they are parked on their own property.

- You can't willfully destroy an old radio.

- No one can sit in the middle of the street and read a newspaper.

Pity the City

Don't do the following in these Michigan cities:

- In Kalamazoo, don't serenade your girlfriend.

- In Grand Haven, you can take it all off, but you cannot
  throw your hoopskirt into the street after you do. They'll
  fine you five bucks.

- In Harper Woods, you can't paint a sparrow to look like a parakeet.

- In Port Huron, emergency vehicles must not exceed 20 mph.

- In Rochester, all sunbathers must have their swimsuits inspected by the police.

State Tour-de-Farce

The state gets into the action, too. Be aware:

- Michigan State law declares that a woman's hair is her husband's property.

- No woman in Michigan may raise her skirt more than six inches when stepping over a puddle.

- Married couples must live together or go to prison.

- A three-cent bounty is paid for each starling and a ten-cent bounty is paid for each crow killed in any village, township, or city in the state. Each rat's head brought into a town office within the state is also eligible for the ten-cent bounty.

CURSING CANOEIST

In 1999 Timothy Boomer of Roseville was convicted of cursing in the presence of women and children after falling out of his canoe on the Rifle River. The 105-year-old law, which nobody ever recalled having been enforced before, drew much applause from moralists and cries of outrage from supporters of free speech. It was repealed in 2002.

Hometown:
Michigan's "Little Bavaria"

*There's Christmas cheer all year in this popular
tourist town with a distinctive German atmosphere.*

The Town: Frankenmuth
Location: Southeastern Saginaw County
Founding: 1845
Current Population: 4,800 (est.)
Size: 2.7 square miles

What's in a Name? The town was settled in 1845 by 15 missionaries from Neuendettelsau, Germany. Frankenmuth gets its name from Franken—the province the settlers came from—and the German word *muth*, or "courage." Simply put, Frankenmuth means "Courage of the Franconians." And courageous those early settlers had to be as the journey from Germany to Michigan was treacherous and their mission—to convert the Chippewa tribe members to Christianity—was far from easy.

Claims to Fame
From 19th century mission colony to present-day "Michigan's Little Bavaria," Frankenmuth draws some three million visitors

annually from every state and over 30 countries. If lederhosen and brightly decorated Christmas trees displayed in the middle of July don't come to mind when you think of Michigan . . . think again. Surprisingly, one of the state's biggest tourist attractions looks more like a quaint German village than a typical Michigan burg—a village with more Christmas gifts and glitter than anywhere outside of Santa's workshop. This town boasts the most authentic Bavarian architecture outside of the Black Forest region. Bavarian flower boxes, a magnificent 50-foot glockenspiel, Michigan's largest wooden covered bridge, a giant maypole, and North America's largest onion-shaped tower make you feel as if you've stepped back in time as you watch candy makers, woodcarvers, leather toolers, wool processors, and sausage makers practice their trades.

Deck the Halls

Frankenmuth features more than 100 specialty shops, but it is most famous for Bronner's Christmas Wonderland, the world's largest Christmas store. Open year-round, the store boasts a two-acre showroom with over 50,000 trimmings and gifts. Each year Bronner's visitors purchase more than 1.3 million ornaments, over 700,000 feet of garland, nearly 100,000 postcards, and over 135,000 light sets. Think your holiday bills are high? Bronner's electric bill averages $900 per day!

Food, Glorious Food

Frankenmuth also claims to be America's chicken dinner capital. The town's most visited eateries, the Bavarian Inn and Zehnder's Restaurants, have a combined seating capacity of

2,500 and serve over 700 tons of famous Frankenmuth-style chicken dinners, over 2 million dinners annually. There's a lot more to see—and eat. The Frankenmuth Taffy Kitchen features a nonstop taffy pulling machine in the window, the Frankenmuth Fudge Kitchen creates 19 delicious flavors right before your eyes, and the Frankenmuth Cheese Haus sells over 120 kinds of domestic and imported cheese.

Beer lovers, take note: Frankenmuth is celebrated for its Oktoberfest, with authentic beer imported from Munich; its annual World Expo of Beer, offering more than 150 beers for sampling; and February's popular Snowfest at the Frankenmuth Brewery, featuring an Outdoor Ice Bar. So raise your beer stein and drink a toast—*ein prosit*, as they say in German—to fun times in Frankenmuth.

UNIQUELY BRONNER'S

- Over 500 styles of nativity scenes, including a life-size nativity, 350 decorated trees, and 150 styles of nutcrackers

- Gifts from 75 nations, including Bibles in 90 languages

- Three super-sized 17-foot Santas and a giant 15-foot snowman

- 100,000 sparkling lights illuminating Bronner's Christmas Lane

- 6,000 styles of ornaments, including "Merry Christmas" greeting ornaments in over 70 languages

- A replica of the chapel in Oberndorf, Austria, where "Silent Night" was first sung on Christmas Eve 1818. "Silent Night" is sung at Bronner's in 263 different languages.

Museum Mania

*The Great Lakes State has plenty of museums to keep
you busy. Here are some of the more unique ones.*

The Nun Doll Museum, Indian River

In 1964 Susan Rogalski opened up her collection of 230 nun
dolls to the public. Now containing over 525 dolls, the collection represents more than 217 religious orders in North and
South America. In 1988 Pope John Paul II blessed her and her
husband Wally "for helping to promote vocations to the priest-
hood and religious life through their doll collection." Located
near the Cross in the Woods Shrine, a National Catholic
Shrine, you'll also have the opportunity to pray before the giant
28-foot-tall crucifix with its seven-ton bronze Jesus.

Marshall Postal Museum, Marshall

The brainchild of postmaster Mike Schragg, the museum opened
in 1987 and is the second largest of its kind in the United States.
Located in the basement of the town's U.S. Post Office, it depicts
the changes in the postal system over the last 150 years and displays postal artifacts like uniforms, mailboxes, and railroad mail
sacks. Highlights include displays of varied postal vehicles and a
re-created post office storefront of the 1890s.

Marvin's Marvelous Mechanical Museum, Farmington Hills

Marvin Yagoda owns and operates his marvelous museum, which began as a hobby but blossomed into one of the most unusual museums in the United States. The arcade/museum boasts 5,500 square feet of historical and modern arcade machines, sideshow wonders like gypsy fortune-telling machines from the early 1900s, singing stuffed animals, futuristic hologram machines, the "world's largest" slot machine, carousels, sideshow posters, and even an original spotlight from Alcatraz. Admission is free, but bring plenty of coins—all of the mechanical marvels are fully operational.

Sindecuse Museum of Dentistry, Ann Arbor

Located in the University of Michigan's School of Dentistry, the Sindecuse Museum of Dentistry houses more than 10,000 items that chronicle changes in dentistry from the late 1700s through the 1960s, both in the operating room and on the battlefield. The museum even houses two historical "operatories," one re-creating the 19th-century pre-electric period when patients' mouths were poked and prodded by candlelight in conditions that are shockingly primitive by today's standards, while the other re-creates the advances made possible by electricity.

DID YOU KNOW?

Detroit native Arnold F. Willat revolutionized the world with a single product. He developed the cold permanent wave process for creating curly hair.

"I Am a Ford, Not a Lincoln"

When most people think of Ford and Michigan, they think
of Henry Ford. But another Ford made his mark on
the state and the country: Gerald R. Ford.

First a King, Then a President

Born on July 14, 1913, in Omaha, Nebraska, to Leslie Lynch
and Dorothy King, Gerald Ford was initially named Leslie
Lynch King Jr. His parents separated two weeks after his birth
and Gerald and his mother moved in with her family in Grand
Rapids. In 1916 his mother married a paint salesman named
Gerald R. Ford. From then on, her son was referred to as
Gerald R. Ford Jr, although it took them until 1935 to legally
change his name.

In his youth, Ford achieved the Boy Scouts' highest rank,
Eagle Scout. It remains one of his proudest achievements. Even
after he became president he unabashedly declared, "I am the
first Eagle Scout President!"

He Sure Could Handle a Pigskin

Ford excelled at his studies as well as in athletics, particularly
at the game of football. While at South High School in Grand

Rapids, Ford was named to the honor society and placed on the "All-State" and "All-City" football teams. His scholastic and athletic prowess continued at the University of Michigan. Ford was part of the Wolverine's championship teams of 1932–33 as well as being voted MVP for the 1934 season. He received offers from the Detroit Lions and Green Bay Packers, but chose to pursue a law degree at Yale instead. After Yale, Ford returned to Michigan where he passed his bar exam, set up a law practice, and taught business law at the University of Grand Rapids.

With the onset of World War II, Ford joined the naval reserves and served aboard the light aircraft carrier *USS Monterey* in the South Pacific as an athletic director and officer in the gunnery division. He returned home in 1946 with a rank of lieutenant commander.

Fate Threw Him the Presidency

Ford's military experiences spurred him into political action. With the backing of his stepfather, himself a county Republican chairman, Ford squared off against the incumbent isolationist representative. Ford firmly believed that an internationalist should represent Michiganders; his war experiences made him realize that the United States was part of a global community. Ford won the election for the House of Representatives in 1948. He served the people of Michigan in that capacity for 24 years before becoming Richard M. Nixon's vice president in 1973. But when Nixon resigned on August 9, 1974, Gerald Rudolph Ford became the 38th president of the United States. Watergate and Vietnam had shattered the nation's trust, and Ford faced the difficult task of healing a nation in crisis.

Ford was also known as the "klutzy" president. He famously became locked out of the White House while walking his dog, Liberty. The Secret Service had to let him back in. Similarly, he was caught on camera numerous times, either tripping or stumbling into people. He became the butt of regular jokes and presidential parodies, most notably by Chevy Chase on "Saturday Night Live" in the late 1970s. His goofiness continued to be gently lampooned decades after his tenure on shows like "The Simpsons." Despite all this, Ford took the ribbing with good humor and even befriended Chevy Chase.

In spite of the many jokes, President Ford went on to accomplish some major acts of diplomacy.

Top 5 Ford Legacies

1. Ford granted President Nixon a full pardon.

2. He provided aid to both Israel and Egypt to ease tensions in the Middle East.

3. He increased détente with the Soviet Union and set limits for nuclear weapons.

4. Ford withdrew the last of U.S. personnel from Vietnam in April 1975.

5. He was the first president to visit Japan.

And the Ford name will forever be a part of his Michigan community.

He's an Airport

Today another Ford is inextricably linked with Michigan. In 1999 Kent County International Airport in Grand Rapids was rededicated as Gerald R. Ford International Airport, in honor of the 38th President of the United States. It is currently Michigan's second busiest airport.

He's a Library and a Museum

Michigan is also home to the prestigious Gerald R. Ford Library in Ann Arbor and the Gerald R. Ford Museum in Grand Rapids. Both facilities comprise the Ford Presidential Library and were opened to the public in 1981.

He's Also a School

In 1999 the Gerald R. Ford School of Public Policy at the University of Michigan was named in his honor and continues to be one of the best schools of public policy in the nation. Perhaps the only major "Ford" name not associated with the president in Michigan is that of the Ford Motor Company. However, he could very well own one.

FORDISMS

"I know I am getting better at golf because I am hitting fewer spectators."

"I watch a lot of baseball on the radio."

"I had a lot of experience with people smarter than I am."

"When a man is asked to give a speech, the first thing he has to decide is what to say."

Superstitions 101

Central Michigan University has some interesting superstitions. If you're superstitious, you might want to check out the first spot with a special someone and avoid the second—especially around finals week.

Cold Kiss

In the 1950s Central Michigan University (CMU) was purported to provide the setting for a tragic love story. It mirrored some crucial elements of Romeo and Juliet with a rich young man, a poor young woman, and parents who just didn't understand. Despite parental objections, the man followed his heart and proposed to his love. The couple arranged to meet in front of the school seal later that night and elope.

As if even fate was conspiring against them, it turned out to be the coldest midwinter night recorded in a decade, made worse by bitter winds and snow. The young Juliet arrived at the school seal on time, but her Romeo was delayed by the inclement weather. By the time he arrived, it was nearly midnight. The wind and the cold had been too much and she had frozen to death. Distraught, the man took her lifeless body into his arms, kissed her frozen lips, and as the clock tower struck midnight, succumbed to his grief and the elements.

This tragic tale has a happy ending, for it is said that the couple was reunited after death. Nowadays, it is said that those who "seal" their love with a kiss in front of the school seal at midnight under a full moon will find their relationship blessed by the lovers.

Whirlin' Skirlin' Widdershins

On the north end of campus is a brick circle with special powers. Wary students avoid it, while the unknowing and unsuspecting tread across it every day. According to superstition, students who break the circle on the way to a test will find themselves failures: answers will escape them, essay questions will become obtuse, and mathematical formulas will turn to gibberish before their eyes. Many a student has fallen victim to the curse during final exams. The only way to reverse the curse is to walk widdershins—that is, counterclockwise—all the way around the circle, starting at the point where the circle was broken.

DID YOU KNOW?

A proper christening is said to bring good luck to a ship, so the *Edmund Fitzgerald* may have been doomed from the start. The ship was christened—and launched—on June 8, 1958, in front of 10,000 people, but it took three tries to break the champagne bottle. The *Fitzgerald* then slid sideways into the water, causing an enormous wave that pushed the ship violently back onto the pier, causing one person to have a heart attack.

Curious Cars

*Henry Ford is regarded as the man who made cars available
to the average American, but other car manufacturers
played a role in popularizing cars and making them
accessible to an ever-widening customer base.*

It's a Horse! It's a Car! It's . . . Both?

Uriah Smith, a Seventh Day Adventist minister and editor in
Battle Creek, Michigan, had a sideline as an inventor. In 1899
he claimed that his Horsey Horseless Carriage Company had
produced an automobile with a wooden horse head in the front
to prevent real horses from getting startled. It is not known if
Smith sold any of his inventions, but in any event this attempt
at bringing the auto industry into the modern world was a flop.

Steaming Ahead

Ransom Eli Olds, later an automotive pioneer, had a shaky start.
Olds was the head of the Olds family's carriage manufacturing
business in Lansing. He later moved his operations to Detroit.
In the 1880s, when steam-powered automobiles were still in
vogue, Ransom designed and built some steam-driven cars. A
gasoline engine heated the water for steam. By modern standards, these steam-powered cars had some drawbacks, namely,

an inability to go in reverse and the need to replenish the water every ten miles. Still, Olds managed to sell one of his steam cars to a British company in Bombay, India. Olds biographer George S. May says that this sale "appears to be the first purchase of a Michigan-made self-propelled passenger vehicle" and "might possibly have been the first foreign sale of an American-made car." It's unclear whether the car was actually delivered to its destination however—Olds later claimed that the steam car sunk en route to Bombay. His point may merely be that the steam car had some value for a time and was not the dodo that it sounded like. Regardless, the steam car was eclipsed in 1896, when two Detroit businessmen independently created America's first gasoline-powered cars.

Give It Some Gas!

First was Charles Brady King, an engineer who also made gas engines for motorboats. King and Oliver E. Barthel, one of his mechanics, drove their creation down Woodward Avenue in Detroit in March 1896, the first appearance of an automobile on the Motor City streets. King never sold any of his cars, in contrast to the other businessman who also produced a gasoline-powered engine that same year, Henry Ford.

Ford devised the 500-pound Quadricycle, a vehicle resembling an open, horse-drawn carriage, mounted on four bicycle wheels. With no horse, but a gas engine, Ford's contraption was steered by a lever like a boat's tiller, within reach of the driver. The Quadricycle was Ford's first car, and its success paved the way to the founding of the Ford Motor Company in 1903. Ford's wildly successful Model T, launched in 1908 and manufactured through innovative mass-production techniques, enriched Ford and came to symbolize the dawning automobile age.

Ransom Olds began work on a gasoline-engine car around 1894. He achieved a breakthrough with his Curved Dash Runabout. Lighter, cheaper, and less mechanically complicated than most previous models, the Runabout was a key stage in the auto's transition from a luxury for the rich to a mass consumer product. It was successful enough to give Michigan the status of a key auto-making area. The Runabout even inspired a popular song called "In My Merry Oldsmobile."

To publicize his Runabout, Olds had one of his employees, Roy D. Chapin, drive it from Detroit to New York to show at the New York Automobile Show in October 1901. Driving to New York by way of Ontario, Chapin found that the terrible roads were damaging the car. Though constantly forced to stop and make repairs, he completed the trip. In addition to garnering good publicity for the car, the trip helped highlight the need for better roads.

Get Behind the Wheel of a Coffin?

It wasn't long before Chapin, along with three other former Oldsmobile employees, set up a new company to take advantage of the expanding auto market. Most of the money for the new company was put up by Joseph L. Hudson, a Detroit department store magnate. In a departure from industry tradition in which the car was named after its designer, this car was called the Hudson. Why? The designer's name was Howard Coffin and "Get behind the wheel of a Coffin" was not a slogan calculated to appeal to customers. The Hudson sold well under its less threatening name. In 1919 the Hudson Company put out a cheaper version of the Hudson—the Essex. The Essex was the first inexpensive American car to be closed like a buggy. Both the Hudson and the Essex succumbed to consolidation in the auto industry. In 1954 the Hudson Company merged with Nash to form American Motors.

In My Rickenbacker Car

World War I flying ace Eddie Rickenbacker, a former race-car driver, used his experience and notoriety to start the Detroit-based Rickenbacker Motor Company, which produced its first car in 1922. Aimed at high-end consumers, the cheapest version sold for the then high price of $1,428. To promote his car, Rickenbacker flew around the country recounting his wartime exploits. The car had no distinctive features beyond a radiator ornament based on Rickenbacker's air unit insignia, the Hat in the Ring Squadron. But in 1924 a four-wheel brake was introduced—its first use in a mass-produced passenger car. Rival manufacturers, whose cars had two-wheel brakes, placed hysterical ads claiming that the newfangled four-wheel brakes would lead to the car overturning or throwing its occupants through the windshield. This propaganda offensive and an economic slump caused Rickenbacker to resign; his company soon went under. Shortly thereafter, four-wheel brakes became standard in the industry. A legacy of the Rickenbacker was one of the earliest love songs to a car. "In My Rickenbacker Car" included such romantic lines as this: "And she's not a bit expensive like most sweethearts are / Always there when I need her, all I do is feed her / It's my Rickenbacker car. Oh car."

Let Them Eat Pancakes!

*Not too many people can say that pancakes helped save their
lives. Here is the story of 200 who might be able to make that claim.*

Back in the late 1930s, the small town of Glenn, Michigan,
was primarily a summer resort, and few people lived there
during the winter. But one three-day period back in 1937 the
population swelled by about 200 people.

Let It Snow

On December 7 it started to snow so hard and so fast that even
the road plows were stuck. Near Glenn, ten-foot drifts stranded
more than 100 cars and 60 trucks, and drivers holed up in the
town's only restaurant and gas station. As the blizzard continued, the town school was opened to stranded motorists and
soon even local residents were taking people in.

Going Like Hotcakes

It continued snowing and snowing. Food supplies began to run
low and soon the only rations available were from the small
grocery owned by Orrin and Betty Burch. A delivery truck had
recently made a delivery and the shelves were stocked full of
dry goods, including pancake flour. With the help of local cows

that provided the milk, travelers stranded in Glenn ate pancakes—for breakfast, lunch, and dinner. For three days!

Pass the Syrup

News of the town's hospitality spread across the nation. The next year, Glenn held a pancake festival to commemorate the event. And the guest of honor? Aunt Jemima, of course. The pancake festival continues, nearly 70 years later, in commemoration of the blizzard of 1937. So the next time you're summering in Glenn, be sure to bring a fork and an empty stomach.

DID YOU KNOW?

- Delaware, Michigan, experienced a record snowfall in the winter of 1978–1979—391.9 inches fell.

- The coldest recorded temperature in Michigan was 51° F.

- The hottest recorded temperature was back on July 13, 1936, when temperatures hit 112° F. That was a year before the blizzard in the accompanying story!

- To cool off you could visit one of Michigan's more than 150 waterfalls and take a walk in the woods—90 percent of the Upper Peninsula's land is forested.

Hemingway Country

Hemingway's books are filled with the heroics of sportsmen and soldiers. Hemingway's manly outlook as well as some of his most acclaimed stories were inspired by the north woods of Michigan.

Ernest Hemingway was born in the Chicago suburb of Oak Park, Illinois, in 1899 to Dr. Clarence and Grace Hemingway. The family spent their summers at Bear Lake (later Walloon Lake) in Michigan, near the tiny havens of Petoskey and Harbor Springs. Grace named their lake retreat Windemere after England's Lake Windermere, popular with the romantic poets. Windemere was actually just a rustic cabin with a wood stove and a water pump. Some of their neighbors were from the Ojibway tribe. A dedicated sportsman, his father taught young Hemingway how to hunt and fish. Ernest favored the rugged Michigan summers over his Illinois school days. In Michigan's wilderness, he had some independence and earned respect as a superb fisherman and a crack shot.

Hemingway described his upbringing in Oak Park as "full of wide lawns and narrow minds." As he grew older, his father pushed him toward a career in medicine. In 1918, when he was 18, and before the United States entered WWI, Ernest volunteered as a Red Cross ambulance driver. He served briefly in

France before being sent to the Italian front. Shortly after his arrival he was wounded in a mortar attack. It was reported that he took over 227 pieces of shrapnel in his body. As he was being evacuated he also took bullets in his shoulder and leg. Ernest returned home to a hero's welcome, limping and with an Italian medal for valor. But he soon left Oak Park. His parents did not understand their son's dark moods or why he wanted to bum around Michigan camping, fishing, and writing stories—stories they thought no one would ever want to read. Fortunately, his parents, who never encouraged his writing, were wrong.

In one of his most acclaimed stories, "Big Two-Hearted River," Nick Adams, psychologically damaged by war, finds a healing sanity in a day of trout fishing. The inspiration was Hemingway's own fishing trip on the Fox River, in Seney, Michigan, after his return from the war.

Going Wild in Michigan

Today Hemingway's fans journey to northern Michigan, to experience firsthand the people and the country that the Nobel Prize–winning author brought to life.

Nick Adams is Hemingway's young, autobiographical hero, a doctor's son who thrives on fishing and hunting in northern Michigan. Like the author, Nick goes off to war as an ambulance driver. When he returns home, Nick suffers from post-traumatic stress—whether Hemingway suffered those mental problems is a topic of debate.

The Nick Adams stories were written and published as individual works over a span of ten years. Some were written after the author completed his famous WW I novels, *A Farewell to Arms* and *The Sun Also Rises*. Most were written after Hemingway married and moved to Paris in 1922. He never returned to Michigan, but it continued to inspire him long after his departure.

Hemingway Country

Because of his attachment to Windemere and its environs, along with its appearance in his work, the area is known as "Hemingway Country." Plenty of places boast, "Hemingway was here." Here are some Petoskey sites where Hemingway left his mark:

- **Little Traverse Historical Museum.** Mentioned in his story "The Indians Moved Away," the building houses a Hemingway exhibit.

- **The Stafford Perry Hotel.** Hemingway stayed here briefly in 1916 after a fishing trip. Every October the hotel hosts a "Hemingway Weekend," sponsored by the Michigan Hemingway Society.

- **Eva Potter's Rooming House.** In the winter of 1919–1920, Hemingway rented a room here to escape his family and to work on his first novel, *The Torrents of Spring*.

- **Jesperson's Restaurant.** A Hemingway hangout that may have inspired the setting for "The Killers."

From Petoskey, it is a short drive to tiny Horton's Bay, which Hemingway described as "only five houses on the main road."

- **Horton Bay General Store.** Hemingway bought supplies at the store, described in "Up in Michigan." Its walls display Hemingway-related photos and news clippings.

- **Pinehurst.** Hemingway often visited this cottage owned by family friends Jim and Liz Dilworth. His family was stunned when one of Hemingway's most sexually frank stories, "Up in Michigan," had characters named Jim and Liz Dilworth.

- **Horton Bay Creek.** Hemingway loved to fish here, once catching 64 trout in one day. The creek runs through "The End of Something" and "The Indians Moved Away."

- **The "Indian Camp"** where the Ojibwa once lived is now private property, but it was here that Hemingway made the friends who inspired the story of the same name.

- **Windemere**, a private home, is still owned by Hemingway's family and is not available for tours. Located on Lake Grove Road, it became a National Historic Landmark in 1968. This was the cottage where Hemingway came each summer for 22 years—except for the summer he spent in Italy. Hemingway and his first wife, Hadley, spent their honeymoon at Windemere in 1921. Windemere also features in several Nick Adams stories, including "The Doctor and the Doctor's Wife," "Ten Indians," "The Indians Moved Away," "The Last Good Country," and, fittingly, "Wedding Day."

"There is no friend as loyal as a book." The man knew something!

Hometown:
A Little Town on the Way Up

This small town in southeastern Michigan attracts visitors worldwide who want to claim they've "been to Hell and back."

The Town: Hell
Location: Livingston County
Founding: approximately 1841
Current Population: 270 (est.)

What's In a Name?

No one knows for sure, but there are multiple theories on the origin of the name. The first claims that German tourists described the area as Hell, which in their language meant bright and beautiful. Another theory suggests that local river traders gave the town that infernal name, frustrated by its challenging passage and swampy conditions. The most popular explanation centers on town founder George Reeves, who, when asked what the town should be called, reportedly said, "I don't care, you can name it Hell if you want to." He later tried to change its moniker to Reevesville or Reeve's Mills, but he was unsuccessful.

Claims to Fame:

- People flock to town every April 15 so they can send the IRS their tax returns with a "Taxes from Hell" stamp and official Hell, Michigan, cancellation.

- Many visitors are drawn by its nefarious name. Some come to tell friends they've been to Hell and back. Others make the trek in winter to see Hell frozen over.

- Hundreds of motorcycle riders converge on Hell every May for its "Blessing of the Rides," which heralds the start of the riding season and the chance to sport a "Blessing in Hell" bumper sticker. Local clergy, typically riders themselves, give the nondenominational blessing at three mass gatherings. Individual blessings also are available. It's a great ride along twisting roads flanked by towering trees and pristine lakes. Business owners lend support with music and a "Taste of Hell" food event. Alcohol is prohibited at many events to ensure Hell is a family-friendly destination.

- Hell has a mission statement: to be "the year-round Halloween theme area in the U.S." Visitors can enjoy frosty treats at Screams Ice Cream or dine at Dam Site Inn located on Hell Creek.

- Before you leave, grab a souvenir. Choose from deeds to a square inch of Hell, ashes-to-ashes ashtrays, Go2Hell license plates, Coffee from Hell mugs and even a degree from Damnation University.

Motown's Greatest?

*Everyone has their favorites, but here are our picks of some
standout songs, and a bit of background about their stellar
performers who made Motown a recording industry phenomenon.*

"Where Did Our Love Go" (1964)

Ross plaintively sings "Baby, don't leave me," while the other
Supremes coo in the background—a classic heartbreaker. This
archetypal Motown girl group featured Diana Ross, Mary
Wilson, and Florence Ballard. Begun as the Primettes, a female
counterpart to The Primes (aka the Temptations), the quartet
signed with Motown in 1961. In 1963 the group, now a trio,
had its first top-40 hit followed rapidly by five consecutive
number-one singles in 1964 and 1965, beginning with "Where
Did Our Love Go." Things began to sour in 1967 with the
ousting of Ballard. In 1970 Ross left to pursue a solo career.

"Uptight (Everything's Alright)" (1965)

This song represented a comeback for Stevie Wonder at the
tender age of 16. Wonder was a true musical prodigy and a
multi-instrumentalist by the age of nine. In 1961, at age 11,
Wonder signed with Motown and a year later had his first hit,
"Fingertips, Part 2" (the song's album, *The 12 Year Old Genius*,

was also Motown's first number-one album). In the following years Wonder was eclipsed by other Motown stars, but this track, (cowritten with Sylvia Moy), showcased his talents as a hitmaker and helped him earn back his place as one of Motown's musical geniuses. In the 1970s Wonder took control of his music from Motown and released some of the most influential R&B albums of all time, including *Talking Book, Innervisions,* and *Songs in the Key of Life.*

"Ain't Too Proud to Beg" (1966)

Sort of the flip side of "Where Did Our Love Go," in this gospel-tinged number, singer Eddie Kendricks acknowledges that his girl wants to leave and declares that he is willing to "beg, plead for sympathy." The Temptations (David Ruffin, Otis Williams, Paul Williams, Melvin Franklin, and Eddie Kendricks) came into being in 1964. The group soon had its first top-ten hit with "The Way You Do the Things You Do," the first of 37 top-ten hits. The firing of Ruffin in 1968 for missing a performance began an era of personnel changes that left the group with only one original member—Otis Williams—in the 1990s.

"Reach Out (I'll Be There)" (1966)

This number-one hit perfectly combined the Four Tops vocal talents with the Holland-Dozier-Holland songwriting machine. Originally called the Four Aims, the group—Levi Stubbs, Abdul "Duke" Fakir, Renaldo "Obie" Benson, and Lawrence Payton— changed their name in 1960 to avoid confusion with the Ames Brothers. The lineup stayed constant from 1953 through 1997, when Payton died of cancer. After a brief stint at Chess Records, the Four Tops joined Motown in 1963. When paired with Brian and Eddie Holland and Lamont Dozier, they started producing hits, starting with "Baby I Need Your Loving" in 1964.

"I Second That Emotion" (1967)

The slow groove rocks in the background, while Smokey sings about refusing one night of kissing and loving from a sweet lady—but says "if you feel like giving me a lifetime of devotion, I second that emotion." Smokey Robinson & the Miracles were the cornerstone of Motown; the band's 1960 hit "Shop Around" introduced the nation to the Motown sound. The label's most consistent hitmakers, they had over two dozen top-40 hits in the 1960s. At the center was Smokey Robinson's romantic tenor and his hit-writing skills. (He also wrote number-one hits for Mary Wells and the Temptations.) Robinson left the Miracles in the early 1970s, with parts of the band continuing with limited success afterward.

"I Want You Back" (1969)

The Jackson 5's first number-one song is a textbook example of their sound: call-and-response vocals between little Michael's falsetto and his deeper-voiced brothers: Jackie, Tito, Jermaine, and Marlon. Signed to Motown in 1968, they opened for Diana Ross the following year. Their first four singles all went to number one, making them the first group to pull off that feat. The Jackson 5 disbanded in 1976 when they left Motown. They became the Jacksons and recruited another brother—Randy—but faded from the limelight once Michael's solo career took off.

"What's Going On" (1971)

Background chatter and mellow sax lead into Marvin Gaye's gentle tenor, describing a world in trouble and imploring those who would "punish me with brutality" to "talk to me, so you can see what's going on." One of Motown's undisputed geniuses, Gaye signed on in 1961. He churned out some minor hits before cracking the top ten three times in 1965, once with "How Sweet It Is (To Be Loved By You)." His 1968 hit "I Heard It Through the Grapevine" may be Motown's single most recognizable hit, but his 1971 album *What's Going On*—a reaction to the era's troubled times—is his greatest triumph. Motown head Berry Gordy didn't "get" it and refused to release the album at first, but eventually relented.

FUNK BROTHERS

What do nearly all the great Motown songs have in common? The backing band, known as the Funk Brothers. These studio musicians stood behind all the Motown greats from Smokey Robinson to Marvin Gaye, and yet until the documentary *Standing in the Shadows of Motown* (2002), directed by Paul Justman, they were as anonymous as their songs were classic. This film goes a long way toward bringing the Funk Brothers into the spotlight for the first time, as the group's members reminisce about playing a role in the most influential music ever to come out of Detroit—and some of the greatest American music of all time.

From Hell to Zilwaukee

In Michigan it's possible to go to Hell and Bach and reach
Climax, Bliss, and Nirvana without ever leaving the state. Here's
a look at some of Michigan's most colorful city names.

Hell

Ironically enough, Hell, in southeastern Michigan, is just east
of Eden. In the mid 1800s this was a rowdy town of whiskey
stills, taverns, and gambling, and was notorious for its drunken
brawls. Anyone going there really was going to Hell, and the
name stuck. And, because this is Michigan, Hell regularly
freezes over.

Temperance

The wife of the first postmaster was also the head of the local
Women's Christian Temperance Union. Liquor was prohibited
and deeds to lots in the town prohibited its use.

Christmas

On the cold shores of Lake Superior, Christmas was named
by a man who started a factory to make Christmas decora-
tions. Businesses use a Christmas theme year-round.

Colon

Trying to come up with a good name, the town's founder opened a dictionary and saw the word *colon*. He thought it appropriate because the river and nearby lake were shaped like a colon. Colon is known as the "Magic Capital of the World" because it is home to the world's largest manufacturer of hand-made illusions, Abbott's Magic.

Climax

Some town names reflect the mood of the early settlers. Climax climaxed the pioneer's desires for a place to settle.

Bliss

Bliss was not a state of mind. The name honored Michigan governor Aaron T. Bliss.

Nirvana

Nirvana's first postmaster admired Buddhism and thought Buddhism's highest heaven was an appropriate name.

Battle Creek

Events that seemed important at the time are still preserved in town names. Battle Creek was named for a battle that was nothing more than a fistfight between two members of a survey crew and two Native Americans.

Crapo

It's not unusual for a town to be named after a state's governor, unless that governor's name is close to a vulgar term for excrement. The townspeople of Crapo, named after Henry H. Crapo, Michigan's governor during the Civil War, must get tired of the jokes and the mispronunciations. It is pronounced KRAY-po.

Maybee
Maybee doesn't reflect indecisiveness over the place. Abram Maybee was the local sawmill owner.

Germfask
Germfask has nothing to do with germs. The town founders took the unusual tack of arranging the first initial of the last name of each of the eight founding settlers into an anagram to come up with the word *Germfask*.

Ypsilanti
Named after the Greek general Demetrius Ypsilanti, who made a heroic stand against the Turks in the battle for Greek independence. As a young man, he was so inspired by the American Revolution that he came to the United States and fought in the Battle of Monmouth.

Ann Arbor
Named after two pioneer women who liked to sit together under a grape arbor.

Zilwaukee
In 1848 the owners of a local sawmill hoping to attract workers came up with the name in an attempt to confuse German immigrants looking for Milwaukee.

Paczki Fever

Described by one Michigander as the "biggest, fattest, richest, most flavorful sweet thing you can have," paczki has become a statewide tradition.

For Christian Poles observing Lent, eating paczki on Fat Tuesday (the day prior to the beginning of Lent) is just common sense. The idea is to get sugar and oils out of the house before the long period of abstinence begins. Pronounced POONCH-key, these deep-fried pastries are loaded with fat and calories (most contain some 420 calories and 25 grams of fat), and over the years they have become just the treat to kick off the 40 days of Lent. In the Polish community of Hamtramck (a suburb of Detroit), Fat Tuesday is also known as Paczki Day.

Hamtramck's Party

In years past Hamtramck crowned a king and queen on Paczki Day and organized a parade to celebrate the holiday, and it didn't take long for the media to get wind of it. In the mid-1980s, when Detroiters began hearing about the pre-Lenten festivities in Hamtramck, people of every ethnicity and religious background began to celebrate Paczki Day along with the little community.

Bakery Fever

Today it seems that everyone in mid-Michigan has an appointment in Hamtramck on Paczki Day. Lines begin to gather outside Hamtramck bakeries before dawn, and only one item is on everyone's minds: paczki. Local bakeries begin making paczki at least 48 hours before the big day, and each one expects to sell upward of 100,000. (Not to be outdone, chain grocery stores participate in the tradition as well. L&L Food Centers in Lansing sell some 240,000 paczki in their nine stores.)

The traditional filling for these popular treats are prunes, but today bakers fill them with just about any flavorful jelly or custard: cream, raspberry, strawberry, lemon, blueberry, chocolate, ricotta, custard, buttermilk, apple, apricot. Not surprisingly, sales of paczki nationwide are now over $650 million, and most of those sales occur during the week of Fat Tuesday.

Ah, Gluttony

Hamtramck has since eased off the formal festivities (it no longer hosts a parade), but the locals, and the town's yearly visitors from around the state, continue to celebrate the holiday. Mostly, that includes eating a lot of paczki and sharing lots more with family and friends. Everyone seems to get in the spirit of the day. Siblings challenge each other to paczki-eating contests, and dieters give up the fight for this one gluttonous day of the year. (One bakery has begun making low-fat paczki that are baked, not fried, but no one has dared commit the sacrilege of creating a low-carb version.) In 2001 the winner of the Hamtramck Knights of Columbus paczki-eating contest ate 13.5 paczki in just 15 minutes.

Battle of the Brans

Direct from Plunges Into Great Lives, *here's the tale of two brothers:
one wanted to fill your bowl; the other wanted to empty your bowel.*

Most people think of bowls—not bowels—when they
think of Kellogg's. Well, think again. Those gr-r-reat
sugar-frosted cornflakes you eat every morning were not what
the good Dr. Kellogg had in mind. It was his younger, more
entrepreneurial brother who had the better idea.

The Doctor as a Young Man
One of America's first health gurus, Dr. John Harvey Kellogg was
born in Tyrone, Michigan, and raised in Battle Creek, Michigan,
with the healthy living tenets advocated by his church, the
Seventh-Day Adventists. Church members helped finance John's
medical school education, and upon graduation he became a staff
physician, then superintendent of his hometown's Battle Creek
Sanitarium. As his influence and ideas rose to national promi-
nence, the institution was renamed the Kellogg Sanitarium.

A Charity Case
John wasn't the least bit interested in riches; his focus was on
sharing his health reform ideas with his colleagues and the

public. He didn't accept a salary at the sanitarium and derived his income from royalties on numerous books and treatises he published. His "rejuvenation" clinic was an elegant combo hotel, hospital, and spa that attracted wealthy health seekers.

No Sex, Please, We're Michiganders

Dr. John had lots of good ideas, including extolling the benefits of a healthy diet, exercise, fresh air, and rest. And he was way ahead of his time in suggesting the link between smoking and lung cancer. But he also had some pretty drastic ideas—like encouraging the excessive chewing of food and opposing any sexual activity—and practiced some quack cures involving treatments with extremely cold water, electric shocks, and mechanical manipulation.

Happy Entrails to You

But nothing fascinated him as much as his obsession with the bowel. He believed that 90 percent of all illnesses could be traced to unclean bowels, and his views became, for a time, a national obsession. He emphasized a regimen that would promote colon cleansing and regularity. His attempts to provide his clients with a palatable and healthful vegetarian diet lead to the next chapter in our story.

The Dark Ages, Cereal-wise

In Kellogg's day, there were few breakfast options and no cold breakfast cereals, believe it or not. Most people ate dry toast or crackers. That is, until Kellogg invented Granola. (What's that? You thought the hippies invented it in the 1960s? Nope. It was created way back in 1881.) Actually, Dr. Kellogg stole another man's invention (and name), of a clustered graham flour product called Granula, and modified the ingredients. When the other inventor sued him, Dr. John renamed his oatmeal-based product Granola. Within a decade Kellogg was selling two tons of the stuff a week. Meanwhile, business at the sanitarium was booming, and by 1888 it had been expanded to add a medical college and accommodate up to 700 patients. (After a 1902 fire, it was rebuilt to accommodate 1,000 guests, attended by an even larger staff.)

Serial Cereal Inventor

Inspired by this success, the doctor created yet another hit—wheat flakes. Again, he "borrowed" someone else's idea. A Denver man had created a product he called Shredded Wheat, little square wheat biscuits. Dr. Kellogg's innovation was the flaking and toasting process. At this point, the cornflakes were still a twinkle in the good doctor's eye, but not far off—give him time.

Kellogg vs. Kellogg

Meanwhile he gave his younger brother William a job as the clinic's accountant. Unfortunately, as is so frequently the case with siblings, they did not always see eye to eye. Battle Creek had been transformed into cereal central and new manufacturers appeared overnight to cash in on the new breakfast fad. Competitors jumped into the cereal market left and right, but Dr. John was only interested in the sanitarium and his medical theories. As for his precious whole-grain foods—he was more interested in playing with them than selling them. His brother, on the other hand, was interested in the bottom line.

Will was particularly annoyed when the cornflake followed the wheat flake and his brother John wanted to name the product Sanitas. Will thought this sounded a little too sterile and unappealing. When his brother took a business trip, Will boldly added sweeteners to the cornflakes. We don't know what inspired this treasonous behavior, but we imagine he was pretty fed up with the whole health regimen of the clinic and his brother's fuddy-duddy ways.

Before you know it, Will was managing the Battle Creek Toasted Corn Flake Company (founded in 1906) and was selling Kellogg's Toasted Corn Flakes under his own name. The two brothers went to court and ultimately Will won. William K. Kellogg built a successful business based on a cereal that tasted better and had a more appealing name than his brother's brands (like the unappetizing Kellogg's Sterilized Bran). Ultimately Will won the right to use the Kellogg's brand name exclusively. Dr. John tried to make a go of the sanitarium but after the stock market crash, his wealthy clientele couldn't afford the luxury of a week or two at a spa.

The Magic Number

Both brothers lived to be 91. But they'd stopped speaking to one another years earlier. To this day, every box of Kellogg's cereal bears W. K.'s signature. But Dr. John earned a place in history too, and is credited with helping foster the development and popularity of such diverse products as the electric blanket, peanut butter, and a menthol nasal inhaler.

Hometown:
Furniture Central

*What do hydroelectricity, furniture, and healthy
teeth and gums have in common?*

Town: Grand Rapids
Location: Kent County
Founding: 1850
Current population: 198,000 (est.)
Size: approximately 45 square miles
What's in a Name? Early French settlers to the area named the
town for the Grand River it was built around. Although the
river's rapids are not big today (as a result of several dams and
fish ladders that have been built on the river), they once
dropped 18 feet in one mile.

Claim to Fame:

- Known as the "furniture capital of America" since the mid-
  1800s, Grand Rapids earned its reputation for fine furniture
  with some 150 furniture companies in town. Recognize the
  brands American Seating, Baker, Sligh, Steelcase, Stickley
  Brothers Co., and Widdicomb? These companies have called
  the furniture capital "home" for more than a century.

- The city boasts the first hydroelectric plant in the United States, which opened in 1881.

- Enjoying your pearly whites? Thank the city of Grand Rapids for starting the healthy-tooth trend. In 1945 it became the first city in the nation to add fluoride to the drinking water.

- The downtown area of Grand Rapids was purchased from the federal government for a trifling sum: $90. The French trader, Louis Campau, bought the 72 acres in 1831.

DAVINCI'S "IL CAVALLO"

In 1482 Ludovico Sforza, the Duke of Milan, commissioned Leonardo DaVinci to build a statue. It was to be the largest equestrian statue in the world. For the next 17 years, DaVinci studied horses and filled his notebooks with drawings of them. Finally, he sculpted a clay model, three times life size. But the sculpture was never cast. The French invaded Italy in 1499 and DaVinci fled for his life, abandoning the sculpture; the French soldiers used it for archery practice.

In 1978 airline pilot Charles Dent read about the horse in a *National Geographic* article and decided to start a foundation. He raised $6 million and hired Nina Akamu, a Japanese-American sculptor, to re-create the statue. She based her design on the sketches in DaVinci's notebooks. The 24-foot-tall statue, *Il Cavallo*, was unveiled in Milan in September 1999. An identical statue was unveiled a month later in the sculpture garden of the Frederik Meijer Botanic Garden in Grand Rapids.

Boy Wonder

*Known as the "Boy Governor," Stevens T. Mason
began his career in public service as a teenager.*

Stevens T. Mason was born in Virginia in 1811, with politics in his blood. Mason's great-grandfather was chief justice of the Virginia Supreme Court and his grandfather and uncle were both esteemed U.S. senators from the state. His father, John T. Mason, moved the family to Kentucky and then to Michigan when he became secretary of the Michigan Territory in 1830. Stevens helped his father navigate backroom politics and in the process learned the nuances of public administration. The son rapidly became a favorite of territorial Governor Lewis Cass, who admired the young man's savvy.

Secretary of the Territory

When John T. Mason was sent on a mission to Mexico in 1831, President Jackson chose his son as his successor, making him acting territorial secretary at the age of nineteen. When Lewis Cass resigned, his position as territorial governor was filled by George B. Porter. Porter served until his death in 1834, but his many long absences left Mason in charge as acting territorial governor, and he became known as the "Boy Governor."

Mason guided Michigan through a cholera epidemic and raised forces for the Black Hawk War, a territorial dispute between American settlers and Native Americans that was threatening to spread from Illinois into Michigan. The "Boy Governor" was also elected alderman-at-large in Detroit and appointed to the highly esteemed Detroit Young Men's Society.

Statehood or Bust!

By 1832 Mason had set his sights on even bigger things: statehood. When Washington turned a deaf ear to his petition, Mason conducted his own census to investigate Michigan's population growth. Although not officially completed until September 1834, the census revealed that Michigan had enough residents to qualify for admittance into the Union. Mason asked the Territorial Council to call a constitutional convention to institute a state government. They agreed to proceed and dates were set for May and June 1835.

Statehood seemed a sure thing until Michigan and Ohio entered into a dispute in 1835 over a 468-square-mile portion of land known as the Toledo Strip. Both sides claimed the territory—owing in part to an ambiguous survey of the region dating back to the Northwest Ordinance of 1787. The ensuing, largely bloodless conflict became known as the Toledo War. Unfortunately it was a war Mason could not win, for while the strip clearly belonged to Michigan, it was Ohio that curried more favor with Washington, thanks to the weight of their electoral votes. When Mason refused to back down, President Jackson removed him from office and stripped him of his duties. Mason's righteous efforts were not lost upon his constituency, who elected him governor later that year. Back in charge, Mason resumed his push for statehood. Congress finally agreed to broker a deal. They would grant Michigan statehood, but only if Mason recognized Ohio's ownership of the Toledo Strip. To sweeten the deal they offered Michigan 9,000 square miles of land in exchange (the Upper Peninsula). Mason conceded the Toledo Strip to Ohio, and on January 26, 1837, Michigan joined the Union.

Ups and Downs

Now firmly in control, Mason began a much-needed internal improvement program, including plans to establish state-supported schools, as well as developing two canals and three railroads. Michiganders were impressed and re-elected him to a second term. Unfortunately, the state's economy began to suffer from the so-called "Panic of 1837," a six-year depression caused by speculative fever. The depression, which was felt across the country, began in May when the banks in New York, the nation's de facto financial capital, stopped payment in silver and gold coinage. The ensuing upheaval crippled Stevens's improvement plans and caused the collapse of Michigan's banking system, resulting in $2 million in debt.

Although his job may have been in jeopardy, Mason's personal life was looking up. He married a young New Yorker named Julia Phelps on November 1, 1838. Alas, a long and happy life wasn't in the cards. Choosing not to seek a third term in 1839, he left politics to pursue a law career. But his successor, William Woodbridge, blamed Mason for the state's financial predicament and charged him with accepting kickbacks on a $5 million loan. Mason attempted to defend himself in court, but the politically motivated allegations—including a false confession that Mason had accepted a bribe—were too much to overcome. In 1841 he left his beloved Michigan for New York City with broken spirits and an empty bank account. He died two years later of pneumonia at the age of 31.

It wasn't until 62 years later, in 1905, that Mason came back to Detroit when his ashes were removed from a New York City crypt and he was finally laid to rest in the city where he made his mark. Present-day visitors can see a statue of Mason as a young statesman standing confidently in Detroit's Capitol Park.

POLITICAL FIRSTS

When it comes to politics, Michigan has been divided between conservatives and liberals since the beginning, as evidenced by these state firsts:

1. Even before suffrage won women the right to vote, Michigan resident Mary Burke won recognition in December 1890 as the first woman delegate to a national labor convention.

2. Michigan led the nation in civil rights for blacks, too. In 1969 Richard Austin was nominated for the office of mayor of Detroit—the first black ever nominated for that office. Coleman Young was inaugurated in 1974 as Detroit's first black mayor.

3. The Republican party held its first convention in Jackson, Michigan, in July 1854.

Do You Speak Michigan?

*If you're a new arrival or a visitor to Michigan, you need
a working knowledge of Michiganisms. Ace this quiz and you're
the genuine article—or at least you can pass as one.*

1. The Big Beaver is:
    A. Big Rapids Dam
    B. Exit 69 off of I-75
    C. The Michigan Environmental Protection Agency

2. The plural of you is:
    A. You all
    B. Yous guys or youse guys
    C. You guys

3. Which of the following are you least likely to find on a
   lunch menu in the Upper Peninsula?
    A. Pasty
    B. Porkie
    C. Cudighi

4. Up North refers to:
    A. The Upper Peninsula
    B. Canada
    C. North of Ohio

5. K-Zoo is:
   A. An annual Lake Superior music festival, sponsored by Radio KZOO
   B. A nickname for the Children's Petting Zoo (Kid's Zoo) in Ann Arbor
   C. Kalamazoo's nickname

6. Which of the following is not shorthand for Ann Arbor?
   A. A^2 (A squared)
   B. AA
   C. Ace deuce

7. Lake Michigan has been called many things, except:
   A. Lake of the Stinking Water
   B. Lac de Illinois
   C. The Gulf of Winnebago

8. Porkies are:
   A. The Porcupine Mountains
   B. Gluttons
   C. Hotdogs

9. Where is the "middle of the mitten"?
   A. The center of Lake Michigan
   B. The center of the Upper Peninsula
   C. The center of the Lower Peninsula

10. Euchre is:
    A. A primary ingredient in a rich winter stew
    B. A popular Michigan pastime—often played at the tournament level
    C. The favored name for off-white or ivory

11. Don't leave home without your Michicard if you want to:
    A. Check out a library book
    B. Withdraw money from a large Michigan ATM network
    C. Cross the Mackinac Bridge at rush hour without digging for change or waiting in a long line
12. Fab 5 refers to:
    A. Five talented University of Michigan basketball players who played two seasons together and twice led the team to the NCAA finals, eventually falling from grace
    B. The Great Lakes: Huron, Ontario, Michigan, Erie, and Superior
    C. The University of Michigan's five campuses

To see how you scored, turn to page 302.

MICHIGAN IS FIRST IN THE UNITED STATES

Michigan leads in auto production, but the state is a vital contributor to the U.S. economy in other areas as well. Michigan ranks first in the production of:

- Potted geraniums

- Pickling cucumbers

- Cranberries

- Blueberries

- Spearmint oil (Did you know that one pound of spearmint oil flavors 135,000 sticks of chewing gum?)

Surfmen, USA

*In the mid-1800s the lighthouse keeper kept the light
on, watched for ships in peril, and rescued men from sinking
ships. As more goods were shipped via the lakes, a
more organized lifesaving group was needed.*

In 1871 Congress funded a professional rescue service—the
United States Life-Saving Service (USLSS)—manned by
brave, strong swimmers who were nicknamed the "Surfmen."
A want ad might have read: "Under 45, able to read and write,
do basic math, and row an open boat across the lake in a
storm."

In its first year of operation on the lakes, workers built 20
lifesaving stations where the Surfmen lived. The second year,
four more stations were built, and by 1900, there were 60 life-
saving stations along the Great Lakes. Most were built near
lighthouses, which had already been situated near the most
dangerous places on the lakes and where the most shipwrecks
occurred. Each station had a keeper who lived onsite year-
round and was responsible for six to eight Surfmen, the
equipment, and the station itself. The keeper was chosen for
his boating skills, as well as his ability to read and write. The
keeper worked all year for his $600–$900 annual salary.

Take This Job and . . .

Surfmen only worked during shipping season, April to mid-December, but they were expected to perform their duties in all types of weather, including those nasty Great Lakes snow squalls. Most Surfmen were paid as little as $2 a day in the mid-1880s, and starting in 1889, they had to buy their own uniforms. A flannel-like coat, with black buttons and a service emblem on one sleeve, warm sweaters, a cap, and overalls were required. Life for the Surfmen was cold and lonely. Days and nights were spent performing drills, hanging out in the watchtower, or patrolling the beaches, looking for ships in peril.

The unofficial Surfmen motto was "You have to go out (in the lake), but you don't have to come back." Accounts claim men dragged half-drowned sailors through high waves one at a time and dodged ice and flotsam in search of missing crewmen.

Ch-ch-ch-changes!

By 1900 improved ship designs and navigational tools meant fewer ships got into trouble or ran aground. In 1915 the U.S. Life-Saving Service joined the U.S. Revenue Cutter Service and became the U.S. Coast Guard. Today's Surfmen (the Coast Guard retained the name for its most expertly trained crewmen and women) are a highly trained, elite group of individuals. They use technology their forebears could never have imagined, but the job remains the same: to save lives.

There is no official estimate of the number of lives saved by the Great Lakes Surfmen, but the Coast Guard claims that over 178,000 people were rescued nationwide in the 44 years of the USLSS.

Magichigans

*Michigan has been a mecca for magicians since the
early 1900s. Thanks to Harry Blackstone and Percy Abbott,
Colon, Michigan, is the "Magic Capital of the World."*

Harry Blackstone and his wife traveled to Colon, where
they purchased a summer home. Harry made many
appearances (and disappearances) around Michigan, wowing
audiences with his tricks. A long-running battle of wits with
rival magician Howard Thurston unfolded during the 1920s.
Gradually, Blackstone gained the upper hand, although it is
rumored that he may have "spirited away" many of his com-
petitor's original tricks. When Thurston accused him of imitat-
ing his assistant-sawing trick, Blackstone responded, "It's true.
I did catch your act in Philadelphia. But you did it so poorly, I
wouldn't try to imitate you."

In 1927 Blackstone invited Australian conjuror Percy
Abbott to his home for a vacation, which resulted in Abbott's
relocation to the area.

The magicians opened Colon's first magic business, the
Blackstone Magic Company, in 1927, but the partnership dissolved when Abbott sold Blackstone's "illusions" along with the
merchandise. In 1934 Abbott opened a new store, Abbott's

Magic Manufacturing Company. He held an open house in 1935, which brought dozens of magicians together to socialize, buy supplies, and watch magic acts. The event was a success and became a yearly tradition. The Abbott's Get-Together is still held every August, and Abbott's Magic has become the world's largest manufacturer of magic supplies.

HOUDINI IN MICHIGAN

World-famous escape artist and mystic Harry Houdini was a frequent visitor to Michigan. In 1906 the escape artist made a particularly dramatic leap into the Detroit River from the 75-foot-high Belle Isle Bridge. Wearing two pairs of handcuffs, Houdini's escape delighted onlookers. Houdini performed at various other Michigan landmarks, including Grand Rapids' Smith's Opera House and Empress Theatre, and Detroit's Temple, Grand, and Garrick theaters.

In Houdini's most famous Michigan feat he was straight-jacketed, handcuffed, and suspended by his ankles from the fifth story of the Grand Rapids Savings Bank. In just under two minutes, the great Houdini had released himself to rapturous applause, thereby securing audiences for his upcoming Detroit tour.

Tragically, Harry Houdini's final connection with Michigan placed him in Detroit's Grace Hospital, where he died of peritonitis from a ruptured appendix after a performance at Garrick Theatre on Halloween night 1926.

Upjohn's Pills

In the 1800s medicinal options were scarce. There was no accurate way to measure doses for mass-producing pills and they did not dissolve easily. Liquids were the medium of choice, albeit a nasty-tasting option. There had to be a better way.

William E. Upjohn was born in 1853, in Richland Township, Michigan, as one of 12 children of a doctor. He graduated from the University of Michigan with a medical degree in 1875 and practiced in Hastings, Michigan, for the next ten years. No stranger to complaints about the pharmaceuticals of the time, Upjohn decided to use his training to try to improve on the current medicinal mediums.

Experimenting in his attic, he came up with a process that compounded bulk ingredients into set dose amounts in pill form. He then devised a machine that built pills layer by layer by spinning powdered medicine in a pan, moistening it, then rolling it around a core. The result: friable pills.

Friable pills crumble easily, making them easily digestible. This was Upjohn's big selling point and he took advantage of it with a unique marketing plan. He sent out samples of his pills to physicians and included samples of his competitors' pills along with a pine board and a challenge: to take a hammer to the pills to see which was more easily crushed—and hence, which would be more easily digestible. In fact, for 60 years after the Upjohn brothers started their business, the Upjohn Pill and Granule Company used a giant thumb squashing an Upjohn pill into powder as its advertising trademark.

Pill Pay Dirt

Upjohn received a patent for his friable pills in 1885, and a year later, he and his three brothers founded the Upjohn Pill and Granule Company in a basement. By the end of 1886, they had developed 186 different medicines and grossed $50,000 in sales. They relocated to Lovell Street and the firm's name was changed to Upjohn Company in 1902. One hundred years later, sales exceeded $2 billion. The reward to the Kalamazoo community where Upjohn lived was just as great.

Hometown Hero

Because of his community involvement, Upjohn was known as Kalamazoo's "First Citizen." He helped institute the commission-manager form of government and, as the first mayor under the new system, wiped out the city's heavy debt burden. He established the Kalamazoo Foundation and the W. E. Upjohn Institute of Employment Research. In addition, he helped fund an art house, a municipal golf course, and the civic auditorium, and donated land for a park.

When he died in 1932, flags in Kalamazoo flew at half-mast and all of the city's businesses and schools closed for his funeral. In 1986 a historical marker was constructed in his honor at the Kalamazoo mall.

Road Shows

Three Michigan attractions will be revealed when you
fill in the blanks. For answers, turn to page 304.

For answers, turn to page 304.

ACROSS

1   Grades 1–12, for short
5   Pause sign
10 Sacramento arena
14 Board's partner
15 Get the better of
16 Spare, as a prose style
17 Sicilian volcano
18 Novelist Calvino
19 Post-op areas
20 East Lansing, Michigan, attraction
23 Chess grandmaster Mikhail
24 Recipe amts.
25 "This foolishness must ___ once!"
26 Blow one's top
28 Nothing but
30 U.S. Open champ Ernie
31 Tick off
32 Sweaters' carriers
36 Annual Trenary, Michigan, attraction
40 Shrinking lake
41 ___ and terminer (high criminal court)
43 Buckingham Palace inits.
46 Keats's work
47 Verdi creation
48 Two or more eras
50 Lady of Spain

53 Brown of renown
54 Ossineke, Michigan, roadside attraction
58 "I'm so sure!"
59 "Wake of the Ferry" painter John
60 Famous Washington office shape
61 High mil. rank
62 100 smackers
63 Native of an ancient country
64 Rowdy party
65 Nathan and Alan
66 Bullfight bravos

DOWN

1   Builder (var.)
2   Lady-killer
3   Capital city near Diamond Head
4   Translucent Apple
5   Stamp rolls
6   Scheduled
7   Deli slices
8   Lounging slipper
9   Early Christian writings not in the NT
10 Weaver flick
11 Retreat
12 Kind of relationship
13 Beginnings
21 Baseball's Mel

22 Wyeth woman
27 Animal-rights gp.
28 Busy as ___
29 Pasternak heroine
32 Prod
33 Kind of log
34 Stacks for eds.
35 Old English poet
37 ___ Perot
38 About eight inches above the shoulders
39 Romantic musical performance

42 Fights, Dogpatch-style
43 ___ at (tried)
44 Paul of "Mad About You"
45 Sharpening
47 It fits in a lock
49 ___ zone (don't go over it)
50 Salivate
51 Kind of marble
52 Lions' locks
55 Novelist Sholem
56 Forearm bone
57 Major ___ (top butler

Smelt Dipping 101

Smelt dipping is one of Michigan's most popular sporting events—after football, of course. It's done between 10 p.m. and 2 a.m. over a three-week period in the spring, when lake water temperatures are between 42° F and 44° F. This is an annual rite for winter-weary Michiganders.

Rainbow, or Eastern American, smelt are small silver-colored fish that reside in the north Atlantic. They were transplanted to inland Michigan lakes in the early 1900s as a food source for larger lake fish. By 1936 the growing smelt population had found its way to the Great Lakes. Commercial fishermen in the area were not pleased, because smelt can clog nets and crowd out other species. But the many new smelt connoisseurs in Michigan could not have been happier.

Fight for Your Right to Party!

Prime time for smelt dipping is mid-April to early May. Michiganders often plan smelt-dipping parties, getting groups of fun-loving folk together for a night in the dark, cold waters. Fortunately for nonanglers, no prior experience is necessary. All you need is a long-handled net, a bucket, warm clothes, and a flashlight. The smelt schools are so large that you merely need to run your net through the water and pull out a swarm of fish. Dump the catch in a bucket and repeat as necessary. Optional equipment: bonfire supplies and lots of beer.

Good Eatin'

What is the reward for all this effort? One of the sweetest, best-tasting fish you'll ever eat. And one of the safest. These youngsters haven't cruised the lakes long enough to absorb mercury or other nasty chemicals. But don't be greedy. You have to clean them before you can eat them, and it can be a chore if you grab too many.

Now that you have a big pile of smelt, what do you do with them? Put them on ice. These delicate critters can turn bad quickly. They also bruise easily, which reduces the quality of the fish, so don't overpack them in large containers. Dress the fish with a pair of scissors.

Many smelt dippers look forward to just one good smelt dinner a year, but any fish that you do not plan to eat right away can be frozen for up to six months.

A Popular Recipe

Dip each fish in a mixture of one beaten egg, half a teaspoon of soy sauce, and half a teaspoon of garlic powder. Roll the fish in flour and cook briefly in a skillet with three or four table-spoons of hot, but not smoking, oil. Then let the feast begin.

Yippee for Yoopers!

Here's a field guide to Michigan's colorful Upper Peninsula inhabitants.

Description. Self-effacing and exceedingly good-humored, Yoopers are among the friendliest folks in the country. Don't let their pleasant demeanor fool you though—they're a rough and tumble sort. Decked out in flannel, sturdy work boots, and a hunting jacket, your average Yooper is ready to hunt, fish, or wrestle a bear at a moment's notice. Yooper genetics are a curious crossbreed of the Finnish, Cornish, Italian, and Irish settlers who came to the U.P. to brave the cold and work the mines in the 18th century. These cultures blended together to form a hardy, sauna-loving community in northern Michigan.

Language. Yoopers tend to draw their vowels out to an almost comedic extent. The letter "o" is generally pronounced as "oooh," while Yoopers pronounce "a" as "ah." Yoopers have an affinity for ending sentences with the word "eh." But the surest sign you're speaking with Yoopers is their insistence on pronouncing "th" as "d." "The" becomes "da," while "them" becomes "dem." Thus, Mackinac Bridge becomes "da crossing" or "da bridge," while the Upper Peninsula becomes "da U.P." or "da Yoop."

Habitat. The U.P. is surrounded by three of the five Great Lakes—Superior, Huron, and Michigan—giving it close to 1,700 miles of uninterrupted freshwater shoreline. Rich with trees, ore, woodland creatures, and natural beauty, it is also a rugged area, with heavy snowfall in the winter and insect infestations in the summer.

Feeding Habits. Over the years Yoopers have developed their own delicacies, which include the biscottilike Trenary Toast—traditional toasted Finnish bread flavored with cinnamon and sugar; the popular pasty—a piecrust turnover filled with meat and carrots (see page 54); and thimbleberry jam. Rumor has it some Yoopers also have a number of different ways of preparing raccoon.

Activities. Yoopers indulge in a number of seasonal activities. The most common winter activities include shoveling out from a massive snowfall (when they're not playing in it) and ice fishing. In the summer they hunt anything that doesn't walk on two legs and swat mosquitoes as if their lives depended on it. Less strenuous activities include taking naked saunas, going for coffee, and supporting Da Pack (the Green Bay Packers). The Detroit Lions belong to inhabitants of the Lower Peninsula, so-called Trolls because they live "below" the Mackinac Bridge.

Field Notes. For those looking to learn the intricacies of becoming a Yooper, there's Da Yoopers School for the Truly Ungifted, an online destination that boasts of being "the only school that learns you good."

Battle Creek's Gr-r-reatest Son

Here's the sweet story of Tony the Tiger,
feline of Frosted Flakes fame.

In 1952 Kellogg's developed a tasty new cereal called Sugar Frosted Flakes of Corn. The product wasn't suited for supermarket shelves without endorsement from a charismatic spokesperson, so Kellogg's asked the people to vote for one of four candidates: Katy the Kangaroo, Newt the Gnu, Elmo the Elephant, and Tony the Tiger. Katy and Tony initially tied, but the tiger's winning personality soon edged out the competition. In 1953 advertising agency executive Leo Burnett presented Tony as the cereal's one and only spokes-tiger.

Tiger Tales

Children's book illustrator Martin Provensen drew the original Tony, but the tiger has gone through a number of cosmetic updates through the years. Tony's trademark growl came courtesy of Thurl Ravenscroft, whose booming bass is also associated with the sneering theme "You're a Mean One, Mr. Grinch." In the 1970s, Kellogg's expanded Tony's presence, making him the spokes-toon for the short-lived cereal spinoffs Cocoa

Frosted Flakes and Banana Frosted Flakes. They also offered a public peek into Tony's private life, introducing wife Mrs. Tony, son Tony Jr. (who got a blink-and-you'll-miss-it cereal of his own in 1976, Kellogg's Frosted Rice), and daughter Antoinette, who was "born" in 1974, the Chinese Year of the Tiger.

Sugar Frosted Icon

At the age of 53, Tony maintains an active lifestyle—and his celebrity shows no signs of diminishing. In 2002 he and Rosie O'Donnell cohosted the Tony the Tiger Award ceremony for outstanding kids, and in 2003 he and Ernie Keebler, "the Keebler elf," acted as cochairs for Michigan Week, an annual statewide celebration. He also presides over regular breakfasts at Kellogg's Cereal City in Battle Creek. And of course there's always Frosted Flakes—with print ads and commercial spots, Tony continues to voice his original opinion of the flakes: "They're gr-r-reat!"

HUMONGOUS FUNGUS

Crystal Falls is home to one of the largest—and oldest—living organisms. In 1988 Myron L. Smith and James B. Anderson of the University of Ontario discovered the 100-ton *Armillaria Bulbosa* while doing research for the U.S. Navy. The mushroom covers more than 38 acres and is believed to be more than 1,500 years old. Though you can buy all kinds of fungus memorabilia in the nearby gift stores, you won't be able to see much of the grand mushroom. Aside from tiny offshoots, it's mostly underground.

A Miller's Tale

*Arthur Miller was one of America's premier playwrights and
he credited the University of Michigan with making him a writer.*

Though he was born and raised in New York City, Arthur
Miller always knew he wanted to study at the University of
Michigan. A friend had told him about the awards that the university bestowed every year on promising writers, and Arthur,
who wanted to be a journalist, recognized this as an indication
not only of the school's largesse, but also of an atmosphere that
respected and nurtured budding scribes.

But Arthur Miller hadn't performed well academically at
Brooklyn's Abraham Lincoln High School. In fact, years later
when he won the Pulitzer Prize for drama, none of his teachers
at Lincoln High even remembered having had him in their
class. Certainly, this was not the way to gain entry into the
prestigious and competitive Ann Arbor school. Nonetheless,
Arthur applied to the University of Michigan for admission but
was rejected because of his poor grades. He reapplied, but was
rejected yet again.

Third Time's the Charm
When he applied to UM a third time, a sympathetic dean

decided to accept him for a year on a trial basis, and he enrolled as a journalism major. To make ends meet, Miller washed dishes at a co-op restaurant and worked as reporter and night editor at the student newspaper, the *Michigan Daily*. In addition, the National Youth Administration, a depression-era agency, paid him $15 a month to feed and clean up after the thousands of mice used for experiments in a cancer research laboratory. Despite all these jobs, he lived on the edge of financial disaster.

Will Write for Money

During spring break of his sophomore year, facing a quickly diminishing bank account, Miller thought about the playwriting awards that had originally kindled his interest in the university. Although his two freshman entries (an essay, "My Private Utopia," and a work of fiction called, *Death and the New*) in the Hopwood Competition didn't even make the first cut, Miller now had to find a way to generate some revenue or face dropping out of school. That turned out to be just the motivation he needed.

Over the course of six days, sitting in his boardinghouse room at 411 North State (just north of Huron), Miller wrote his first play, *No Villain*. Incredibly, this first effort won the 1936 Hopwood Award in drama, with its $250 cash prize—a kingly sum in those Depression days. Miller celebrated by running through the streets of Ann Arbor in jubilation. He changed his major to English and never looked back.

Flush with his first success and mindful of the $250, Miller decided to compete again the following year. He wrote a play called *Honors at Dawn,* which also won. He reworked *No Villain* and called it *They Too Arise.* It won an award of $1,250 from the Bureau of New Plays and was produced in Ann Arbor and Detroit. It was beginning to look as though he couldn't lose. He tried for a third Hopwood Award and came very close—his play, *The Great Disobedience,* placed second. Arthur Miller, the kid who almost didn't get in, graduated in triumph in 1938. Though he had his ups and downs, a brilliant career had been launched, and he later went on to great success with his plays, which include *Death of a Salesman*—for which he won a Pulitzer Prize—and *The Crucible.*

A Loyal Wolverine

Miller's relationship with the University of Michigan and Ann Arbor endured through the years. He was a frequent visitor, speaker, and advisor to students. In 1956, the year he married Marilyn Monroe, he was awarded an honorary doctorate from his alma mater. In 1985, in recognition of the financial help he received from the university and the National Youth Administration, he established the Arthur Miller Award for Dramatic Writing to help other aspiring dramatists at Michigan. "The Hopwood Awards were very important for me and, I think, a lot of other people," Miller said at the time. "It's important for morale, because writing is a lonely profession."

In October 2000, in honor of Miller's 85th birthday, the University of Michigan staged an international symposium on his work, and broke ground for a new theater bearing his name. Miller told the university that it was the only theater in the world to which he would lend his name.

Birth of a Giant, Part III

By now you know that the patent for the first modern bathtub spawned General Motors. But whatever happened to Billy Durant and David Buick? Read on. (Part II begins on page 107.)

Comeback

The bank-appointed executives who took control of GM from Billy Durant made a number of moves that helped restore the company to health. They shut down all of the money-losing divisions and used the money they saved to improve quality at Buick, Oldsmobile, Cadillac, and other divisions that showed promise. In just a few years, they rescued the company from the brink of bankruptcy, paid back all bankers, and built GM into one of the most competitive U.S. auto companies.

But the executives made a mistake that would cost them dearly. They discontinued the Buick Model 10, a low-priced Buick that Durant had created to compete against Ford's Model T. Shortsighted GM executives were skeptical that smaller, cheaper cars would ever make any money. (The Model T would become the best-selling car in American automobile history.) So they scrapped the Model 10, despite the fact that it was the most popular car in the Buick lineup, and concentrated on building bigger, more expensive cars.

The decision was a disaster for Buick: sales at the division dropped more than 50 percent in one year, forcing GM to shut down entire assembly plants and lay off hundreds of workers.

See the USA

The crisis at Buick gave Durant an opening. In 1911 he bought an abandoned Buick factory, staffed it with Buick auto workers who'd been laid off during the sales slump, and announced that he was forming a new company to manufacture and sell cars designed by Louis Chevrolet, one of the most famous race car drivers of the day.

Some of the larger Chevrolets really were designed by Louis Chevrolet . . . but the new company's best-selling model, introduced in 1915, was basically a Buick Model 10 that had been rechristened the Chevrolet 490 (so named because it sold for $490). Priced just $50 higher than the Model T—but equipped with an electric starter and other features that the Model T lacked—the 490 was poised to give Ford a run for its money.

And thanks almost entirely to the 490, sales at Chevrolet nearly tripled from 5,000 cars to more than 13,500 cars in 1915, making Chevrolet one of the top auto companies in the country. Durant had done it again, and he was only getting started.

He's B-a-a-a-ck

Even as he was building Chevrolet into an automotive power-house, as early as 1913 Durant began secretly acquiring large blocks of General Motors' stock. He encouraged friends and associates to do the same, and even convinced the DuPont Chemical Company to acquire more than 25 percent of GM.

On September 16, 1915, Durant pounced. He showed up at GM's annual shareholders meeting accompanied by several assistants carrying bushel baskets filled with the GM stock certificates that Durant either owned or controlled. "Gentleman," Durant calmly announced to the room, "I now control this company."

Déjà Vu

This time Durant managed to stay on at GM until 1920. He inherited a much stronger, more profitable company than the one he'd left in 1910, but as time passed he began to slip into his old habits. He bought the Sheridan and the Scripps-Booth auto companies and added them to the GM fold, but they did little more than steal sales from GM's other divisions. Durant also bought up several tractor companies and merged them all into what he named GM's Samson Tractor Division, which went on to lose more than $42 million before it was finally shut down in 1920.

Durant might have even managed to survive these debacles had the U.S. economy not fallen into a deep recession in 1920. As sales of automobiles dropped sharply, GM's stock price began to plummet, prompting Durant to buy shares in an attempt to keep the stock price from sliding further. It didn't work—by the time Durant exhausted his fortune in November 1920, GM's share price had dropped from a high of nearly $50 to under $12.

The Birth of Gerber

*Behind every successful man, there's a woman, and
the woman behind Daniel Gerber was his wife, Dorothy, who
also was the founder of today's giant baby food company.*

When the family pediatrician recommended to Dorothy Gerber that she hand-strain their daughter's food to make it easier to digest, her husband, Daniel, offered to help. As Dorothy watched him struggle to produce soft food for their daughter, Sally, inspiration struck. It dawned on her that the equipment at her husband's family-owned business, the Fremont Canning Company, would probably do the job far more efficiently—and with less mess to their kitchen—than Daniel.

After some experimentation, the Gerbers successfully produced strained peas, prunes, carrots, spinach, and beef vegetable soup. Thus, in 1928, the first product line of premade, canned Gerber baby food was created.

Gerber Grows Up

With adept marketing, eager consumers gobbled up the baby foods, and the Gerber product line expanded to take over the entire resources of the Fremont Canning Company. The company name was changed to Gerber Products Company within a year. Over the next 70 years, Gerber launched additional products, including insurance and skin care products for infants. In 1994 the company merged with Sandoz Ltd., and in 1996 became part of the Novartis group of companies, an international conglomerate. But the little town of Fremont, Michigan (population of about 4,000), is still headquarters for the production of baby food that is distributed to more than 20 foreign countries.

The Real Gerber Baby

Sally is not the famous Gerber baby pictured on the products or in advertising. In 1928 Gerber sought illustrations for a national advertising campaign to introduce its prepared baby foods. They hired artist Dorothy Smith, who sketched her neighbor's daughter, Ann Turner Cook, now the world's most famous unknown celebrity.

Playing with Their Food

Each July about 100,000 people attend Fremont's National Baby Food Festival to honor babies and families with five full days of entertainment and, of course, food. The baby food–eating contest is a big draw, but it's only open to those over the age of 18. Participants work in pairs and the people doing the feeding are blindfolded, which means a lot of the food ends up on their partners' faces—just like when feeding babies. There's also a baby food cookoff, in which participants must come up with a tasty treat—for all ages—that incorporates at least one baby food. For the little ones, the festival offers a baby crawl, a kiddie parade, and a midway with rides.

Bragging Rights

Besides being the car capital of the world, Michigan boasts the largest cement plant, the world's biggest registered Holstein dairy herd, and the biggest source of magic supplies. Three more Michigan superlatives are revealed in this puzzle grid. For answers, turn to page 305.

ACROSS

1   Hold up
5   Doctor's charges
9   Charlie Parker's jazz style
14 Bruins' sch.
15 Bar on a car
16 San Antonio landmark
17 Burglar's take
18 Box-office draw
19 Italian bread
20 Rogers City, Michigan, has the world's largest
23 Swimming apparatus
24 Admiral's org.
25 Sardine container
26 Vegetarian's no-no
28 Kimono sash
31 As a result
34 Sweeping story
36 Equivalent to D sharp
38 Michigan produces the most of these
41 Rick or crick
42 Elvis's middle name
43 Dynamic leader

44 Yo-yo, e.g.
45 What's more
47 What Bugs called most people
49 Adherent's suffix
50 Self-serving behavior
54 Michigan produces the most of these
59 Yale of Yale University
60 Course climax
61 Draft classification
62 Passover meal
63 Emulate a balloon
64 In apple-pie order
65 Double curves
66 Summers in France
67 IDs for the IRS

DOWN

1   Quiet periods
2   Flip ___
3   Replay feature, for short
4   Certain spuds
5   Clothespin, e.g.
6   Glorify
7   Distinctive flair

1	2	3	4		5	6	7	8		9	10	11	12	13
14					15					16			
17					18					19			
20				21				22				
23							24					
		25			26	27			28	29	30
31	32	33		34	35			36	37		
38			39			40				
41				42				43		
44			45	46			47	48		
		49			50			51	52	53
54	55	56		57	58				
59				60				61		
62				63				64		
65				66				67		

8 Parched
9 Railing support
10 Cuban headline boy Gonzales
11 Mercury motor Maxima In
12 Actor Epps
13 Nosegay
21 Take to the slopes
22 Sine ___ non (requirement)
26 Prefix with scope
27 Canyon sound
28 TV's Rolie Polie ___
29 Boxer Max
30 "Wishing won't make ___"
31 Once, once
32 Seized vehicle
33 Aussie's "hello"

35 Groups for soccer moms et al.
37 Parts of a whole
39 Green group
40 Chess finures
46 Was in front
48 Ball or bass ending
49 "With this ring ___ wed"
50 Clear, as a blackboard
51 Ancient letters
52 "That is . . ."
53 Early tests for coll.
54 Cash in Cuba
55 Designer Cassini
56 Ocean motion
57 Richard of "Chicago"
58 Way to go

Lasting Impressions

Several sites that contain prehistoric fossils are being excavated in Michigan today. One of the most renowned is the Brennan Site.

In 1992 Harry Brennan began excavating his land in Saline, Michigan, to build a pond for his grandchildren. He watched in awe as a backhoe uncovered the enormous pelvis of a mastodon. Digging for the pond halted and a full-blown archaeological dig commenced. Brennan enlisted the help of Dr. Dan Fisher, curator and paleontologist at the University of Michigan, who unearthed several more fossilized bones and, most astonishingly, a set of mastodon footprints that had been preserved for over 12,000 years.

See for Yourself

The University of Michigan's Museum of Natural History houses a cast of the mastodon footprints taken from the Brennan Site. Called the mammoth trackway, it highlights Michigan's state fossil, the *Mammut Americanus,* commonly known as the mastodon. Linking Michigan's history to our own, the late Cenozoic mammal exhibit boasts that it is the "best record of human association with extinct Ice Age mastodons found anywhere on the continent."

Shafted in Detroit

*For years, thousands of miners toiled deep below
the city of Detroit, but how much do you know
about the vast salt deposits they mined?*

Evaporation of the ancient seas covering Michigan deposited
salt beds throughout the state. In 1906 miners dug a 1,000-
foot shaft into solid salt deposits and began to extract the salt.
In the past 100 years, the extraction of tons of solid salt crystals has left huge tunnels running beneath Detroit and environs. The layer of rock salt closest to the surface is over 1,000
feet down and is 20 feet thick. Mining today is from a second
layer of salt, which is at least 30 feet thick and begins 1,100
feet from the surface. The Detroit mine covers 1,500 acres and
has over 100 miles of roads.

Working in a Salt Mine
In earlier days miners rode a small, six-man elevator down into
the mines. Mules, lowered down into the shaft with ropes,
hauled the salt from digging operations to the shaft for removal.
Equipment had to be disassembled, lowered down the shaft,
and reassembled in the shaft. In more recent times the shaft was
expanded and giant trucks with seven-foot tires have been used

to haul salt boulders to machines to crush the crystals into smaller pieces for removal by conveyor belt. The mine shaft opening is located at 12841 Sanders Street, and miners still access the mine through an elevator cage that plunges almost a quarter-mile down. They exit to an ancient cavern over two stories high.

It's a Blast

The mine consists of an eerie maze of hundreds of rooms and pillars of salt created from the removal of millions of tons of crystallized salt. Because pure salt crystals are very hard, extraction of salt from the earth requires "hard mining" techniques. Workers bore holes in the salt layer and use explosives, made from fuel oil and fertilizer, to blast the salt into large boulders that are then ground to small salt pellets.

When salt is removed, workers leave thick layers of salt on the top and bottom for a hard roof and floor. Wide pillars of salt are left untouched to support the roof, making the mine a series of dark but secure rooms. With no water or gas in the mine, it's actually a safe environment. No employees have been killed since the mine's original construction.

Well-Seasoned State

While Michigan no longer holds the title of the leading salt-producing state in the nation, the Detroit mine pulls out a million tons of rock salt each year. The entire annual production is used to melt snow and ice on roadways. With Michigan's lake-effect winter snowstorms, the demand for road salt won't diminish soon.

The Best Business Deal in U.S. History, Part II

When the Dodge Brothers put $3,000 in cash and $7,000 in parts into the Ford Motor Company, they made history. Here's what happened next. (Part I of the story is on page 75.)

Turnaround

Four weeks after the Dodge brothers made their deal with Malcomson, the Ford Motor Company was on the verge of bankruptcy. With $223.65 in the bank, not a single car sold, and payroll for the Ford workers due the next day, it looked like the company's stock would be worthless.

Then, on July 15, 1903, a dentist named Dr. E. Pfennig became Ford's first customer, paying $850 cash for a Model A. "Dr. Pfennig's payment of the full cash price through the Illinois Trust and Savings Bank represented a turning point in the fortunes of the Ford Motor Company," Robert Lacey writes in *Ford: The Men and the Machine.* From $223.65 onward, its cash flow went one way only.

Up, Up, and Away

When it opened for business in 1903, the Ford Motor Company could only build a few cars at a time. But as orders increased, Henry Ford and his assistants knew that the key to success was to find ways to speed production.

They did. In the fiscal year ending September 1906, the company made 1,599 cars; the following year, production more than quadrupled to 8,000; and by 1912, Ford was manufacturing 78,000 cars per year. That was only the beginning: production more than doubled the following year and then more than doubled again in 1914, until Ford was manufacturing over 300,000 cars per year, or 1,000 cars for every workday, a production increase of 4,000 percent in just over a decade.

Oh, Brother

About the only thing that grew faster than the Ford Motor Company's production and sales figures was the value of Ford stock, ten percent of which belonged to the Dodge brothers. They earned back their entire $10,000 in the first year's dividends alone, and since then their Ford stock has paid out millions more.

In addition, because they were still manufacturing most of Ford's mechanical components at their own Dodge Brothers factory (at the time the largest and most modern such manufacturing plant in the world), they profited twice: first by supplying parts to Ford and second by owning shares in the company.

T-Time

That changed in 1914, when Henry Ford built his own parts manufacturing plant to replace the one owned by the Dodge brothers. Until then, the Ford Motor Company, like most other auto companies, had focused on assembling cars, leaving the actual manufacturing of the parts to subcontractors. Now that Ford could afford to finance his own manufacturing plant, he didn't need the Dodge brothers any more.

With their business relationship with Ford coming to an end, the brothers had to figure out what to do with their plant. Henry Ford had offered to lease the plant and run it himself, and the Dodges gave it serious thought . . . but then they had another idea.

Don't Change a Thing

When it went on sale in October 1908, the Ford Model T was the most advanced car of its day. As the years passed, automotive technology improved, but Henry Ford refused to make any changes to it, stylistically or even mechanically. Unlike other cars, you still had to start the Model T using a hand crank, and because it didn't come with a fuel gauge, the only way to tell how much gas you had was by dipping a stick into the gas tank. Having been with Ford from the beginning, the Dodge brothers knew all of the car's weaknesses, but when they suggested improvements, Ford ignored them.

In the end, the Dodge brothers decided to use their factory to manufacture the car that Henry Ford refused to build: one that was better than the Model T.

Turn to page 222 for Part III.

State of Confusion

Michigan's state flag features a moose and an elk. Its state game mammal is the white-tailed deer. So how come Michigan is known as the "Wolverine State"? Three prevalent stories show how Michigan got its nickname.

In 2004 coyote hunters made headlines after spotting and treeing a wolverine in the woods of Michigan's Huron County. Why was a single wolverine sighting such a big deal in the Wolverine State? Quite simply, it was the first confirmed sighting of a wild wolverine in Michigan history. In Michigan's 168 years of statehood no one had ever trapped a wolverine.

Holy Toledo

Many believe Ohioans gave Michigan its nickname around 1835 during a dispute over the Toledo Strip, a valuable piece of land along the border between Ohio and Michigan. Both sides wanted to control the mouth of the Maumee River, and neither was willing to give in. The dispute escalated into the "Toledo War," and although each side sent militia to the area between 1835 and 1837, no shots were ever fired—it's said that the armies spent most of their time getting lost in the swamps. In the end, President Andrew Jackson gave the land to Ohio in what was perceived as an attempt to curry favor during an election year. (Michigan wasn't a state at the time and thus had no electoral votes. Ohio was and did.)

Despite their victory, Ohioans were so disgusted with the Michigander's vicious and gluttonous behavior that they likened them to wolverines. The name stuck. And so did the rivalry—these days the Ohio State University Buckeyes/ University of Michigan Wolverines football game is the most highly anticipated matchup of the year. The University of Michigan adopted the wolverine for its varsity sports team mascot in 1861. You'd be hard pressed to choose a more menacing mascot. Pound for pound, the wolverine is one of the world's most powerful predators. These vicious animals are capable of bringing down caribou and witnesses have seen them drive wolf packs from their kills.

Fur Sure

Another theory suggests that the name comes from the state's early fur-trading days. Wolverine pelts—of particular value because the animals' natural oils make their fur water- and frost-resistant—routinely arrived in Michigan from all across Canada and the West. This idea was championed by legendary University of Michigan football coach Fielding H. Yost. In the 1944 *Michigan Quarterly Review* he wrote that he believed the state's nickname came from pelts Native Americans in far northern Ontario sent through the fur-trading post at Sault Ste. Marie on route to the East Coast.

Yost's connection to wolverines runs even deeper than that. The coach was responsible for asking Michigan trappers to get him a live wolverine for use as a team mascot in 1921. When none had been caught (or even spotted) two years later, the state had ten shipped in from Alaska and placed at the Detroit Zoo, where they were periodically taken out for University of Michigan football games.

True to their reputation, however, the wolverines became increasingly ferocious and the practice had to be curbed. As Yost reflected, "It was obvious that Michigan mascots had designs on the Michigan men toting them, and those designs were by no means friendly."

Attack of the Mountain Devil

According to others, the nickname originated during the 1830s, when Native Americans compared pioneering Michiganders' lust for land with the wolverine's bloodthirsty pursuit of food. True or not, Native Americans have long believed wolverines to be possessed by evil spirits because of their nasty dispositions and habit of devouring animals caught in trap lines. In fact, Native Americans still refer to the wolverine as "carcajou," a French corruption of a Native American word meaning "Evil Spirit" or "Mountain Devil."

What's in a Name?

No matter which explanation you believe, Michiganders have embraced their identity as the mighty "Wolverine State" since the beginning, proudly displaying the voracious animal on crests, logos, and designs from one end of the state to the other. These days anyone wishing to see a wolverine within Michigan can visit the Detroit Zoo, where they're safely out of reach.

Hometown:
B&B Country

*Popularized by its fame in the art community, this tiny
town on the banks of Lake Michigan is a haven unto itself.*

Town: Saugatuck
Location: Allegan County
Founding: 1830
Current population: 1,050 (est.)
Size: 1.2 square miles

What's in a Name? Saugatuck means "river's mouth" in the
language of the Potawatomi tribe that lived in the area at the
time of its founding. True to its name, the town is built along
the Kalamazoo River, which empties into Lake Michigan.

Claim to Fame:

- The town was one of the few in the area not devastated by
  the fires of 1871. Instead, lumber milled in Saugatuck and
  neighboring communities was used to help rebuild Chicago.

- At Saugatuck, a hand-cranked chain ferry carries pedestrians
  across the Kalamazoo River.

- Saugatuck is unofficially known as the "Bed and Breakfast Capital of the Midwest." Some 38 B&Bs in and around town are popular havens for weary urbanites seeking respite from the pollution and summer heat in nearby metropolitan areas.

- When the Art Institute of Chicago started a summer camp in town in 1914, Saugatuck was introduced to fine art and was soon known as Michigan's "art coast." Today, Saugatuck attracts artists, art dealers, and art aficionados with its picturesque landscape and the Oxbow School of Art and Gallery.

- The sand dunes to the west of town feature spectacular vistas from the top of Mount Baldhead. (Though once bald, the giant dune "Baldy" has been topped with trees to keep it from slowly migrating any further eastward.)

DID YOU KNOW?

Strident abolitionist Carry Nation—along with her handy hatchet—arrived in the town of Holly, Michigan, on August 2, 1908, to set the drinkers and sinners straight. She chopped up bars, broke bottles, and screamed at the wrongdoers. The town was never quite the same again.

In honor of that visit, every September in Holly, Carry Nation rides again. She winds her way down the crowded streets of Holly on the weekend after Labor Day, dressed in an austere, old-fashioned dress, as she sneers disapprovingly at smoking, bars, inappropriate language, tight clothing, and all other "immoral" behaviors. And is that an ax in her hand? Welcome to the Carry Nation Festival!

Official Business

How well do you know Michigan's state symbols?

1. After winning an election held by the Michigan Audubon Society, the robin redbreast became the official state bird in 1931. How many votes were cast?
   A. 20
   B. 200
   C. 2,500
   D. 200,000

2. What's is Michigan's state fish?
   A. Bluegill
   B. Brook trout
   C. Channel catfish
   D. Largemouth bass

3. The apple blossom became the official state flower in 1897. What is its scientific name?
   A. *Angelonia angustifolia*
   B. *Eustoma grandiflorum*
   C. *Iberis umbellate*
   D. *Pyrus coronaria*

4. The mastodon became the official state fossil in 2002. In how many different locations have the fossils been discovered in Michigan?

    A. 45
    B. 160
    C. 250
    D. 300

5. In 1997 a group of fourth graders successfully lobbied for the white-tailed deer to become the official state game mammal. Which county are these fourth graders from?

    A. Huron
    B. Marquette
    C. Niles
    D. Zeeland

6. In 1972 chlorastrolite became the state gem. Its colors range from yellow-green to almost black. What does its name mean?

    A. Flower stone
    B. Green stone
    C. Green star stone
    D. Plant stone

7. When and how did the painted turtle become the official state reptile?

    A. In 1889 the governor's niece proposed that the painted turtle become the state reptile.
    B. In 1930 a zoo lobbied for the painted turtle to become the official state reptile.

C. In 1995 it was selected when a group of fifth graders discovered that Michigan did not have a state reptile.

D. In 2003 the painted turtle became the state reptile because it is the most common turtle in Michigan.

8. The official state soil (out of a possible 500 variations to choose from) is Kalkaska sand. How many acres does this sand cover in the 29 Upper and Lower Peninsula counties?

A. 1 million

B. 5 billion

C. 10,000

D. 50

9. The white pine became the official state tree in 1955. How high is the tallest white pine in Michigan?

A. 115 feet

B. 175 feet

C. 201 feet

D. 275 feet

10. The official state stone, the Petoskey stone, is fossilized coral that existed some 350 million years ago. What is the ethnic origin of the name?

A. Native American

B. Russian

C. German

D. Polish

Turn to page 305 for the answers.

Wheels

Detroit's passion for the car spurred the creation of one of the largest and most extravagant events, the North American International Auto Show.

Every January Michigan residents bundle into their warmest clothing, drive to downtown Detroit and pay homage to the invention that impacts every facet of their daily lives: the automobile. The North American International Auto Show draws 75 exhibitors, nearly 7,000 journalists, and almost 1 million people during its 15-day run. The main attraction is the cars.

Michigan's first auto show was held in 1907. The Detroit Auto Show was held at Beller's Beer Garden at Riverside Park on Jefferson Avenue in Detroit. A total of 17 exhibitors showcased 33 vehicles. The cars, and the adjoining hunting and fishing accessories, thrilled attendees.

As the show increased in popularity, the demand for additional exhibits grew, causing it to move to larger venues three times, from the Michigan State Fairgrounds to the Detroit Artillery Armory before settling at its permanent home, the Cobo Center, in 1965.

The show went international in 1957 when domestic models from the Big Three—General Motors Corporation, Ford Motor Company, and Chrysler Corporation—shared floor space with

Volvo, Isetta, Mercedes-Benz, Jaguar, and Porsche. The show's importance was not lost on the homeland, drawing visitors like President Eisenhower in 1961 and President Clinton in 1999.

International firsts soon gave the show cachet among the foreign press. Toyota introduced its new Lexus in Detroit. Nissan did the same with its luxury line, the Infiniti. What started with a few international reporters now accounts for more than 30 percent of the press credentials issued for the show. Soon the show was filled with overseas carmakers like Hyundai and Mitsubishi. As a result, the name was changed in 1989 to the North American International Auto Show to reflect the growing presence of foreign automakers.

On With the Show

Competition bloomed among the automakers to see who could deliver the most dramatic or luxurious displays. In 1990 Mercedes-Benz added parquet floors to its exhibit. Two years later, Chrysler's president, Bob Lutz, crashed a Jeep Grand Cherokee into the front of the Cobo Center through a special plate glass. Now special effects are commonplace, from virtual-reality simulators to Internet stations that let users design and order their cars right from the show floor.

The show traditionally opens with the annual Charity Preview, aka the "Auto Prom." Automotive executives, media representatives, and anyone else who can score a ticket dress to the extreme, drink champagne, and take in the show before the public. When the event premiered in 1976, it raised $15,000 for local nonprofit organizations; in 2004 it generated more than $7 million.

Putting the show together may be the most impressive aspect of the event. It takes ten weeks to put up the exhibits, which cover every inch of Cobo's 700,000 square feet. More than 1,500 carpenters, stagehands, electricians, riggers, and ironworkers are employed full time to stage the show. Another 1,700 are responsible for the show's daily activities including 65 vehicle polishers, 135 car porters, 200 janitors, and 450 security personnel. Show exhibits are valued collectively at more than $200 million, excluding the value of the cars themselves. The show contributes about $600 million to the southeast Michigan economy.

MICHIGAN MOTORING FIRSTS

- Detroit had the first mile of concrete highway (Woodward Avenue between 6 and 7 Mile roads) in the world in 1909.

- The first drive-in gas station opened in 1910 in Detroit.

- The nation's first painted center lines (River Road near Trenton) were drawn in 1911.

- The nation's first roadside park (on U.S. 2, Iron County) was opened in 1919, and first roadside picnic tables (U.S. 16, Ionia) were constructed in 1929.

- The first state welcome center was opened in 1935 near Buffalo.

- Packard Motor Car Company introduced the first automobile air conditioning in 1939.

- The first urban freeway—the Davison Freeway in Detroit—was completed in 1942.

A Wet Mitten

The state motto—Si quaeris peninsulam
amoenam, circumspice, *which means, "If you seek
a pleasant peninsula, look about you"—applies
equally well to both the U.P. and the L.P.*

Michiganders like to explain where they live by pointing
to a spot on their outstretched right palm. But
Michigan's mitten-shaped peninsula is only half of the state's
land mass. Don't forget the Upper Peninsula!

Head South to Get Up North

Think of Michigan as "up north" and "just south" of Canada?
Think again. Parts of Michigan are closer to the equator than
parts of California and further east than parts of North
Carolina. Check a globe!

And, by the way, when crossing the Ambassador Bridge
from Detroit to Windsor, Ontario, you are traveling due south,
not north. In fact, more than half the population of Canada
lives south of Copper Harbor, Michigan, including the residents of four of Canada's largest cities (Toronto, Montreal,
Ottawa, and Quebec City.)

Life's a Beach

Geographically defined by lakes Superior, Michigan, Huron, Saint Clair, and Erie, Michigan has more beaches and a longer shoreline than either California or Florida. In fact, at 3,288 miles, the state's coastline is longer than the entire U.S. Atlantic seaboard. Some of the best freshwater beaches can be found along Michigan's shores, including the nation's highest sand dunes. (For more on the dunes, see page 29.)

Smack Dab in the Middle

The 45th parallel passes through the Lower Peninsula, placing parts of Michigan exactly halfway between the equator and the North Pole. Due in part to its strategic position in relation to the former Soviet Union, Michigan was home to some gigantic Air Force bases during the Cold War. Those bases housed fleets of B-52 bombers loaded with nuclear weapons.

Water, Water Everywhere

More than four percent of the state's area consists of water. Besides the Great Lakes, Michigan boasts 11,000 inland lakes, 36,000 miles of rivers, and over 150 waterfalls. Wherever you are in the state, you are always within 85 miles of a Great Lake and within six miles of an inland lake.

The Great Lakes—along with a few miscellaneous rivers—create the country's largest inland water transportation route, the St. Lawrence Seaway.

Third Time's the Charm

*On May 15, 1926, Detroit was granted a franchise
in the National Hockey League. The team was called
the Detroit Cougars from 1926 to 1930 and the Detroit
Falcons from 1930 to 1932. The Red Wings name
and winged wheel logo were adopted in 1932.*

12-28-4 The Cougars' regular-season record for the 1926–27 season. It's the worst record in the league and the fewest victories the team ever managed in a season. (The team also won only 12 games in the 1937–38 season.)

1927 The Olympia arena opens.

1927–1963 Jack Adams's tenure as coach/general manager with the team

1928–29 The team has its first winning record (19–16–9) and makes its playoff debut, going 0–2.

12/12/79 Opening night of Joe Louis Arena, the Red Wings' new hockey palace

62 League-record number of regular-season victories by the Red Wings in 1995–1996

48 Red Wings in the Hall of Fame

25 Number of seasons Gordie Howe played for the Red Wings (1946–1947 through 1970–1971)

10 Number of Stanley Cups the team won in its history (through the 2003–2004 season). Only the Montreal Canadiens (24) and Toronto Maple Leafs (13) have won more.

7 Consecutive seasons (1948–1949 to 1954–1955) the Red Wings finished with the best regular-season record in the NHL

6 Number of overtimes the Red Wings played against the Montreal Maroons in a 1936 playoff game. The Wings scored a 1–0 victory after 176 minutes and 30 seconds of playing time. The game ended at 2:25 a.m. As of 2005 it is still the longest game in NHL history.

5 Number of Hart Trophies Gordie Howe won as the league's Most Valuable Player

4 Number of Red Wings' captains who went on to coach the team. They are Art Duncan, Sid Abel, Ted Lindsay, and Alex Delvecchio.

1, 7, 9, 10, 12 Numbers retired by the team (1-Terry Sawchuck, 7-Ted Lindsay, 9-Gordie Howe, 10-Alex Delvecchio, and 12-Sid Abel)

Howe Amazing!

The first family of hockey.

- Gordie Howe's career with the Red Wings nearly came to a premature end. In his first training camp, Howe was promised a team jacket. When the jacket didn't appear in his locker, Howe threatened to go home. General Manager Jack Adams quickly found a jacket to keep his young prospect happy.

- Howe wore number 9 for the Detroit Red Wings, but he was number 1 in just about everything else. By the time he hung up his skates, Howe had set more records in his sport than any other athlete in history.

- Howe is still Mr. Hockey—just ask the United States Patent and Trademark Office. Howe and his wife, Colleen, registered the names Mr. and Mrs. Hockey to use in promoting their charitable foundation.

- Howe played professional hockey for 32 years, longer than Hockey Hall of Fame members Guy LaFleur and Bobby Orr combined.

- Howe won four Stanley Cups with the Red Wings, appeared in 29 all-star games, finished in the top five in league scoring for 20 consecutive years, won six Most Valuable Player awards, and led the league in scoring six times.

- When Gordie Howe came out of retirement in 1973 to sign with Houston in the World Hockey Association, he became the first modern professional athlete to play alongside two sons as teammates.

More Hockey Howes

- Gordie and Colleen Howe's two sons, Mark and Marty, both became stars in professional hockey. They were teammates with the Houston Aeros of the World Hockey Association from 1973 to 1977 and with the New England/Hartford Whalers from 1977 to 1982.

- In 2000 the entire Howe family—Gordie, his wife Colleen, and his sons Mark and Marty—was inducted into the U.S. Hockey Hall of Fame. It was the first time a family was inducted into a major sports hall of fame as a unit.

- Colleen Howe, a Michigan native, has been called "arguably the most influential woman in the history of hockey." She was instrumental in developing junior hockey in the United States.

- The first woman to serve as a player agent, Colleen also became the first woman to be enshrined when the Howe family was inducted into the U.S. Hockey Hall of Fame.

Let the Good Times Roll!

*Take a trip back to the rockin' 1950s
at the Woodward Dream Cruise.*

Woodward Avenue and the burgeoning automotive industry were a match made in heaven. In 1909 Woodward Avenue had the first paved mile of concrete road in the world. In 1920 the world's first electric traffic light was installed at Woodward and Michigan avenues. The street was widened to eight lanes in 1926 between Six Mile Road and Pontiac. By the 1950s the street had grown into a 27-mile stretch of road, reaching from downtown Detroit into the outlying country. It was a cruiser's dream road. Happy days had arrived.

Rock Around the Clock Tonight

Woodward's golden age was in the 1950s and 1960s, captured in the 1973 film *American Graffiti*. On warm nights, Fords, Chevys, and Valiants paraded down the world's most famous cruising strip transporting guys in lettermen's jackets, girls in poodle skirts and bobby socks, and the greasers parents tried to keep their kids away from.

End of an Era

In the 1970s America's first gas crisis brought an end to the good times. Merchants, fearing growing crime rates along much of Woodward, pressed for an end to the last vestiges of the cruising. They succeeded, and cruising down Woodward soon became a memory.

Let's Cruise

Some, however, refused to forget. In 1994 Nelson House and a group of volunteers launched the Woodward Dream Cruise to raise funds for a soccer field. Though not intended to be more than a one-time, one-day fundraising event, it has since grown into the world's largest one-day automotive event and is attended by more than 1.5 million people every year.

Forty thousand classic street-worthy cars cruise 16 miles up and down the historic avenue, which runs through nine communities, including Berkley, Birmingham, Bloomfield Hills, Bloomfield Township, Ferndale, Huntington Woods, Pleasant Ridge, Pontiac, and Royal Oak. Crowds gather along sidewalks—often setting up camp early in the morning—to enjoy the day of nostalgia. Local communities add to the festivities with live concerts, amusement park rides, celebrity appearances, swap meets, manufacturer displays, Elvis impersonators, restaurant rows, and even sock hops and streetside soda shops. More than a decade old now, the Woodward Dream Cruise shows no signs of stopping.

Musical Mystery Tour

A state as great as Michigan needs a state song to sing its praises, but agreeing on one is not as easy as you might think.

For years, "Michigan, My Michigan" was considered the state's unofficial song. Detroit native Winifred Lee Brent Lyster penned the ten-verse anthem in 1862, which is sung to the tune of "O Tannenbaum." Winifred's husband, Henry Lyster, served as a surgeon during the Civil War, and after the Battle of Fredericksburg, she wrote the song, which included many vivid references to "heroes slain" and "strong arms [that] crumble in the dust." It gained popularity with Michigan's Union Army troops, but its gory details made it inappropriate for dinner parties and dances.

In preparation for the semicentennial celebration in 1886, Major James Long of Grand Rapids wrote new words for "Michigan, My Michigan," focusing on the state's attributes, such as "the lake-bound shore," and scaling back on the battle gore, while still paying homage to the "noble sons" who "bit the dust."

On a More Peaceful Note

Yet another songwriter wrote different lyrics for a 1902 convention of the Michigan State Federation of Women's Clubs in Muskegon. Deemed more suitable for peacetime, Douglas Malloch and William Otto Miessner's version, scaled down to four stanzas, is still performed at club meetings, state conventions, school events, and patriotic musical gatherings. This version gained so much notoriety that most people think it is the state song, though it has only received the "official" designation by the Michigan State Federation of Women's Clubs, not the state legislature.

It Could Be Verse

"My Michigan," penned by lyricist Giles Kavanagh and composer Harold O'Reilly Clint, came close to being declared the official song. Clint had already composed several official songs—"Step by Step" for the American Legion Department of Michigan and "Shoulder to Shoulder" for the Veterans of Foreign Wars Department of Michigan.

Early in 1937 "My Michigan" was proposed to the legislature for designation as "the official song of the state of Michigan." The Committee on Rules and Resolutions deliberated and the resolution was passed on May 21, with the language altered to deem the tune not "the" official song, but "an" official song. Although it did not reach the pinnacle of honor, it is the only song with the designation "official" to its name.

DID YOU KNOW?

There is enough pavement in Michigan roadways to build a one-lane road from Earth to the moon.

The Big Mac

The Straits of Mackinac divide Michigan's upper and lower peninsulas. Across this turbulent five-mile span arcs the Mackinac Bridge. The building of the Mighty Mac is a story of human ingenuity and determination in the face of towering odds.

Calls for a bridge to unite the upper and lower peninsulas began as early as 1884. Advocates maintained that a bridge would unify a state that had long been split by politics, culture, and economy and bring needed tourism dollars to the Upper Peninsula. Despite enthusiastic support, the bridge was not completed for another 73 years.

The Straits of Mackinac posed daunting obstacles to bridge construction: strong currents, huge ice sheets in the winter, and fierce winds during storms. Early studies reported that the bridge could not be built. In addition to technical challenges, citizens and political supporters failed for years to secure the massive funding required.

Although private companies offered car ferry service across the Straits, it was costly and unreliable, especially in the winter. In 1923 the State Highway Department launched its own ferry service, and usage rose so sharply that the governor ordered a bridge-building study. The 1928 report said that a bridge could be completed for about $30 million. But before the state could find the needed funds, energy to build the bridge fizzled out and historical records do not provide clues as to why.

In 1934, eager for federal funding, the state legislature created the Mackinac Straits Bridge Authority. The Bridge Authority was empowered to explore bridge feasibility and was authorized to finance, build, and operate the bridge. It presented the federal government with two distinct proposals, each about $35 million and both rejected as too costly. Undeterred, the Bridge Authority continued to push the project forward. The Authority made soundings and borings; studied traffic, geology, ice, and water currents; built a 4,200-foot causeway; and drew up plans for a double suspension bridge.

In November 1940 disaster struck. Just four months after it opened, Washington's Tacoma Narrows Bridge collapsed into Puget Sound. Fortunately, no one was killed, but the design of the Tacoma Narrows Bridge was strikingly similar to one proposed for the Mackinac. Indeed, one of Tacoma's engineers also worked on the Mackinac design. The disaster cast a chill over the Michigan project. Still, the Mackinac scheme might have proceeded if the United States had not entered World War II in 1941. The Bridge Authority put its plans on hold.

Bridge Authority—Lost and Found
The legislature lost interest in building the bridge and abolished the Bridge Authority in 1947. Instead, it approved funds to build a new ferry. In 1949 a citizens' committee urged the state to restore the Bridge Authority and in June 1950 these efforts succeeded. But the resurrected body was empowered

only to study feasibility, not to pay for or build the bridge. In 1951 the Bridge Authority submitted a report to the legislature prepared by three of the world's top experts on long-span bridges. It outlined plans to use the existing causeway. The Bridge Authority also asked for restoration of its former powers. Finally, in April 1952, the governor signed Public Act 214. It gave the Bridge Authority the power to issue bonds to finance construction and then to build and operate the bridge. By 1953 the Bridge Authority had $99.8 million to cover building the bridge; bridge tolls and gas and license plate taxes would pay for its operation and maintenance.

Groundbreaking ceremonies were held in May 1954. The completed Mackinac Bridge opened to traffic on November 1, 1957—a mere three and a half years after construction began.

The Lessons of Tacoma

Engineers who analyzed the collapse found that the bridge's solid girders had blocked the wind. Therefore, when heavy winds swept through Puget Sound, the Tacoma twisted, buckled, and, finally, broke. For the Mackinac, engineers designed both the trusses and large portions of the suspension span with open steel grating to allow wind to pass freely through the bridge. The trusses that stiffen the Mackinac are extraordinarily wide and deep to enhance stability. The Mighty Mac remains strong and sound, a monument to those who kept alive the dream of bridging the Straits of Mackinac.

How Does It Measure Up?

At the time it was completed, the Mackinac was the longest

suspension bridge in the world. At 8,614 feet (including anchorages), it remains the longest suspension bridge in the Western Hemisphere. (The longest suspension bridges in the world are Japan's Akashi Kaikyo Bridge (12,826 feet) and Denmark's Great Belt Bridge (8,921 feet).)

The 1,024,500-ton bridge includes 931,000 tons of concrete, 71,300 tons of structural steel, 11,840 tons of cable wire, 4,851,700 steel rivets, and 1,016,600 steel bolts. The bridge's towers (552 feet high) are almost as tall as the Washington Monument (555 feet tall). Its main cables are made from 42,000 miles of wire, with 12,580 wires per cable.

The Mackinac had a huge impact on traffic across the Straits. In 1957, the last year the state offered ferry service, crossing the Straits averaged 1.5 hours in winter and 2.5 hours in summer, including wait time. A bridge crossing took just ten minutes no matter what the time of year. In one hour a ferry could carry up to 462 cars, while the bridge could take as many as 6,000 cars. The Bridge Authority marked the hundred millionth crossing in 1998. Some 1,752,930 cars crossed the bridge in 2004 alone.

DID YOU KNOW?

The expression "the real McCoy" came about because of Elijah McCoy, a Michigan Central Railroad employee. The son of escaped slaves, he studied engineering but went to work as an oilman for the railroad. He designed a can that would safely deposit oil where it was needed and applied for a patent, the first of 50 he took out during his lifetime. His products were so good, people would ask for "the real McCoy."

Octopi on Ice

The Detroit Red Wings are one of the oldest franchises in the NHL. In existence since 1926, they have won a total of ten championships and produced such great players as Gordie Howe, Danny Gare, and Steve Yzerman. They are also famous for an unusual annual tradition.

For nearly 53 years, fans of the Red Wings have kept an eight-tentacled tradition alive; the throwing of octopi onto the ice during playoff series. As far as sporting traditions go, this one is a bizarre spectacle that has left sports fans outside the Motor City scratching their heads in confusion.

Humble Origins

On April 15, 1952, fishmongers Pete and Jerry Cusimano flung the first octopus (boiled, not live) onto the ice of Olympia Stadium (where the Red Wings played at the time). Back then, the NHL playoffs could only be won by achieving eight victories over two rounds of play. Basically teams needed to first win four games out of seven to advance past the semifinals, then another four games out of seven in the finals to be crowned champions. Thus, the symbolism behind the Cusimanos' choice of object; each of the octopus's arms represented one of the wins needed to capture Lord Stanley's Cup. Octopi have lived in mortal fear of Red Wings fans ever since.

Getting Out of Hand

This tradition has spawned a kind of competitive one-upmanship over the years. In 1995 fans heaved a 38-pound octopus onto the playing surface while the national anthem was being sung. The next year, not to be outdone, fans managed to haul a whopping 50-pounder onto the ice. No one is sure how that one got through security.

Not everyone is a fan of the tradition. Animal activists, marine biologists, and others have decried the tradition as cruel. Yet the tradition continues and isn't likely to end any time soon. According to the Michigan Humane Society, no one has complained about this activity in the last few years. However, in an effort to curb octopi-tossers, the Red Wings organization has installed a 30-foot, purple Styrofoam octopus in the rafters of the Joe Louis Arena, which is lowered onto the ice during the pregame ceremonies to assure the team's good luck.

DID YOU KNOW?

The Portage Lake ice hockey team, organized in 1899 in Houghton, became the world's first professional hockey team.

Berry Gordy Jr.

How much do you know about the man behind Motown?

Berry Gordy Jr. was torn between becoming a boxer and becoming a musician. A high school dropout, he divided his time between writing songs and training under future Hall of Fame trainer Eddie Futch, who would train Larry Holmes, Riddick Bowe, Michael Spinks, Joe Frazier, and Trevor Berbick. Berry showed talent as a featherweight fighter, but eventually decided against the life of a brawler.

The Early Years

After a stint in the army during the Korean War, Gordy came back to Detroit and opened the 3-D Record Mart, a jazz music store. The shop closed in 1955 and Gordy worked the line at a Lincoln-Mercury plant during the day to support his wife and children while he wrote songs at night. Gordy's sister Gwen introduced him to local music manager Al Green, who in turn introduced Berry to R&B star Jackie Wilson. In 1956 Wilson had a hit with "Reet Petite," a song Gordy cowrote, so he purchased more songs from Gordy, which also became hits. Eventually a quarrel over royalties ended that relationship. By then, however, Gordy had established himself as a hitmaker and was on his way to founding Motown.

In 1959 Gordy bought a house at 2648 West Grand Boulevard in Detroit, which Gordy, with no lack of hubris, dubbed "Hitsville USA." Upstairs was the Gordy family living quarters; downstairs was the music studio and business offices of the newly formed Motown Records. The first song written and recorded at Hitsville was the Gordy-penned "Money (That's What I Want)," recorded by Barrett Strong, which became a hit in 1960. Gordy's connections with Smokey Robinson (who became a Motown VP) and other local singers and songwriters made the modest building on West Grand Boulevard one of the most musically historical buildings of the 20th century. Some of Motown and R&B's most famous names recorded here. The building is now the Motown Museum.

Motown Style

While Motown's artists were almost exclusively African American, Gordy wanted to make his label's music appeal to the widest audience possible. To that end Motown actively managed the appearance and presentation of all its artists to maximize their appeal. The label hired elegant jazz singer Maxine Sullivan for Motown's "Finishing School" to groom the label's young performers for stardom and give them some idea of how to comport themselves in public. Motown had a "look" as well as a sound.

Music, Money, and Movies

Royalty disputes were at the heart of a falling out that damaged

Motown's success. The dispute involved the songwriting trio of Brian and Eddie Holland and Lamont Dozier, who penned some of Motown's greatest hits in the 1960s. The songwriting team was indisputably a cornerstone of Motown's huge success, but by 1968 the team felt that Gordy was withholding royalties and they left Motown to form their own Los Angeles–based Hot Wax and Invictus labels. Motown scholars point to their departure as the point where Motown's fortunes began to fall, although—to be fair to Gordy—the fall was a very slow one. Gordy moved to Los Angeles in 1968, and in 1972 he moved his entire Motown operation west and expanded its operations to include movies, as well as music. Films Motown produced include *The Wiz* and *Lady Sings the Blues*. By the mid-1980s, the label's luster had fizzled, and Motown was losing millions of dollars annually. In 1988 Gordy sold the label to MCA for $61 million.

Motown Roll Call

Motown's roster reads like an R&B hall of fame: Stevie Wonder, Smokey Robinson, the Temptations, the Supremes, Marvin Gaye, the Jackson 5, the Commodores, Rick James, DeBarge, Boyz II Men, and Queen Latifah are just a small sampling. But Motown was more than R&B. It was an umbrella company for over 40 labels specializing in everything from blues to country and western music. Believe it or not: one label, Melodyland, had Pat Boone as its featured artist. Between its various labels and artists, Motown managed over 60 number-one hits in the United States in the 20th century.

Take a Michi-gander at This

Here you go, Michigan fans—31 of your fine state's cities and towns worked every which way into this state-shaped word search. If you find 'em all, feel free to make your own much larger version with all the towns we had to leave out!

ADRIAN	LIVONIA
ALBION	MARQUETTE
ALPENA	METZ
ANN ARBOR	MIDLAND
BATTLE CREEK	MONROE
BAY CITY	MOUNT PLEASANT
BIG RAPIDS	MUSKEGON
BIRMINGHAM	NILES
CADILLAC	OWOSSO
DEARBORN	PONTIAC
DETROIT	SAGINAW
FLINT	TAYLOR
HOLLAND	WYANDOTTE
KALAMAZOO	YPSILANTI
LANSING	YUMA

```
        P N                          F
      A L R T Y                    N Z I
    N O G E K S U M            O Y Z T L M Y
R O T X F C F L M C T    Q M A R Q U E T T E X P
M O U N T P L E A S A N T D M E U M S R W F G
      T I X K T O D R                  S
      N X C F                          S
      T A                            T M Q
      P                          B R A I B E
                                 Q H U D C T A
                    F            G H O L L A N D
              Q        N F R B A C C N T
            P L S F I G N P O N T I A C
            C A F D M O N R O E D T U R X
            P L N R O B R A E D N R E B Y
          B O A I C F T A X Y A Z L T O R
          C R B A I N O V I L L T U F R          E
          C D T A Y L O R P I M X E O Y      T F
          A J A K F E J Z S J O E S L    T C X
          S A G I N A W P M N T S      O Y K J
            L E I T P Y J C U O      D A B M E
            K W X F E D R E W G N I S N A L U R X
            Z N I L E S S O Y W T E A Z F I Z C Y
            Y X E J D M L O P Q K Y T I C Y A B
            D W P I L T P Z H I W N U K T L Y
            E Y P H S A Z A P Y N O I B L A
            T A L P E N A M Y I B L E I T
          E M R X N A I R D A S Q Z F D T
          Q G O C H J I T I L M N Z A X
        R I X I F J F N M Q A R R C L R
      L B A T T L E C R E E K E Y R A B
```

For answers, turn to page 306.

The Best Business Deal in U.S. History, Part III

Here's the last installment of the
story. (Part II is on page 187.)

Car Wars

On November 14, 1914, the first Dodge rolled off the assembly
line. It had a bigger engine than the Model T and a modern
stick-shift transmission, as well as features like a speedometer,
an electric starter, electric headlights, a windshield, and a spare
tire. And it only cost $100 more than the Model T.

The Empire Strikes Back

Naturally, Henry Ford was not amused that Ford dividends
were being used to bankroll his competition. But when the
Dodge brothers offered to sell him their Ford stock, he refused
. . . and instead announced in 1916 that the Ford Motor
Company would no longer pay dividends and would instead
plow all of its profits back into the business.

The Dodge brothers sued to force Ford to pay dividends,
and in 1919 they won: Ford was required to pay $19 million
in back dividends (most of which went directly back to him,
because he owned the lion's share of the stock anyway), but

he would not give in. In December 1918 he announced that he was "retiring" from Ford and turning control over to his son Edsel.

Henry left for an extended vacation in southern California. Then on March 5, 1919, the *Los Angeles Examiner* broke a story that shook the automobile industry:

HENRY FORD ORGANIZING HUGE NEW
COMPANY TO BUILD A BETTER, CHEAPER CAR

According to the report, while his old company had employed 50,000 workers, the new company would hire as many as 250,000 and would have automobile plants all over the world. The scale of production would make it possible to sell cars for between $250 and $350, cheaper than they had ever been sold for before. No other auto manufacturer would be able to match the price.

Getting Out

The Dodge brothers were in a bind—if Ford was serious, the new company would probably drive both the Dodge Brothers and the Ford Motor Company out of business. Their own company and their Ford stock would be worthless.

"But the Dodge brothers and the other minority shareholders found themselves mysteriously approached in the following weeks by would-be Ford share purchasers," Robert Lacey writes. "It became clear that the threads all led back to Henry, working through Edsel in Detroit. The bidding started at $7,500 per share (the Dodge brothers owned 2,000 shares). The Dodge brothers responded with their $12,500 price—and

$12,500, in the end, became the price that Ford had to pay."
The "huge new company," it turned out, was just a ploy that
Ford used to depress the value of the Dodge brothers stock so
that he could buy them out on the cheap.

So Long, Fellas

The Dodge brothers received $25 million for their Ford stock,
which came on top of the $9.5 million they had received in
dividends between 1903 and 1919, for a total return of $34.5
million on their original $10,000 investment. Even though
Ford had received the better of the bargain, the Dodges (along
with the other original investors in Ford) made so much
money that business historians now consider it the most profitable investment in the history of American commerce.

Note: Less than a year later, the Dodge brothers were attending
the 1920 New York Auto Show when Horace suddenly fell ill
with pneumonia. His condition was so grave that John maintained a round-the-clock bedside vigil, only to catch pneumonia himself and die ten days later. Horace lingered for just a
few more months before he died. In 1925 their widows sold
the Dodge Brothers Motor Car Company to a New York banking syndicate for $146 million in cash—at the time the largest
cash transaction in auto history. In May 1929 the bankers sold
Dodge Brothers to automaker Walter Chrysler for $170 million
. . . just in time for the Great Depression.

Yo Ho Ho and a Barrel of Venison

Long after piracy's golden age in the West Indies, the waters of Upper Michigan remained a swashbuckler's paradise.

Today, the Upper Great Lakes Region is a tourist's and hunter's paradise, but during the late 19th century, it was a dangerous place. Renegade boatmen stole equipment and tackle from fellow seafarers. Hordes of "timber pirates" illegally clear-cut private lands. Lawless captains filled their boats with Canadian liquor and unloaded it in ports from Houghton to Detroit—then filled their holds with American firearms to sell in Canada.

While history provides many tales of brigands performing small-time deeds of mischief and misdemeanors along Michigan's coasts, the most notorious Great Lakes pirate was "Roaring" Dan Seavey. Operating in the early 20th century, his exploits earned him a place in folklore as "Michigan's Lone Pirate": Escanaba folk singer Carl Brehrend immortalized him in "Dan Seavey, the Great Lakes Pirate."

Seavey was born in Portland, Maine, where as a youth he learned to sail. After a brief stint in the U.S. Navy, he relocated to Milwaukee, Wisconsin, where he unsuccessfully tried his hand as a professional fisherman. Broke, Seavey headed north to Escanaba, Michigan. It was in this thriving harbor community that Seavey's activities became somewhat less wholesome.

A Pirate's Life For Me

In Escanaba, he assembled a crew and stole a schooner that he christened the *Wanderer*.

Seavey's widely recounted exploits involved everything from petty theft to trafficking in contraband, but many historians believe that Seavey himself was responsible for spreading some of the taller tales. Seavey and his crew were experts in one endeavor—venison poaching. They would poach deer on secluded Beaver and Fox islands, as well as the coastal wildernesses around Escanaba, Manistique, and St. Ignace. Sometimes they would even steal preprocessed meat from port warehouses! Once their holds were full, they sailed to Chicago to unload the stolen meat for a profit. Venison shipping was serious business in northern Michigan. When another "shipping company" tried to cut in on the action, Seavey fired a cannon at the other vessel, killing everyone on board.

Seavey's crew also practiced a form of piracy known as "moon cussing." This practice involved setting up false harbor lights in treacherous waters. Vessels who thought they were sailing into a safe port, instead ran aground, whereupon the *Wanderer* would arrive, kill everyone, and steal the ship's cargo.

Whoa, Nellie!

"Roaring" Dan Seavey's most celebrated exploit was the commandeering of the *Nellie Johnson*, a Charlevoix-based schooner.

One evening Seavey came upon the docked vessel and invited the crew to join him for a drink. The sailors drank until they were completely incapacitated. Everyone that is but Seavey, who ended the party by tossing the drunken sailors out of their own vessel and single-handedly piloting it out of the harbor.

Seavey took the *Nellie* to Chicago, where he sold its cargo. Upon leaving, however, he was found by the cutter *Tuscarora* in pursuit. He evaded the authorities for several days, but their dogged pursuit inspired him to resort to some impromptu moon cussing. He shot out a buoy light and placed a lantern on top of an empty beer barrel. Falling for the trick, the *Tuscarora* ran aground, but even after crashing, she attempted to fire on the *Nellie*, which Seavey had piloted out of range.

But Seavey, perhaps distracted by his success, didn't look where he was going and smashed into a dock. The *Nellie* was lost and Seavey was caught. Although put on trial for the heist, he was released unsentenced. The owner of the *Nellie Johnson* not only failed to appear to testify, but also seemed to have vanished from the area. Michigan's Lone Pirate escaped his closest encounter with the law.

A Kinder, Gentler Pirate

The most unbelievable turn of Seavey's career comes at the very end of it. He was hired as a United States marshal to curb poaching and robbery on Lake Michigan! Why would this long-time harbinger of havoc and purveyor of stolen goods go to work for the government? The answer is lost to history. Whatever the reason, Seavey's story is one of the few pirate legends with a happy ending.

Which Michigander Am I?

*Can you guess the identities of these notable
Michiganders from the clues provided?*

Michiganders have made their mark in every field of human endeavor because they are just that good. Following are clues about some particularly notable folks who were born or lived in Michigan. Can you guess who they are from the information provided?

1. I am an actress from Detroit who gained fame in the 1970s as the straight girl of a crazy alien played by a now-famous comedian. I am married to the son of Wolverine football legend Tom Harmon. Who am I?

2. I am a doctor and an inventor. My most famous invention is an artificial heart, the first one that allowed its owner to survive for more than a few days. The first person to receive this heart lived for 112 days in 1982. I'm still working in the field and recently created a heart pump the size of a thumb. Who am I?

3. I was born in New Jersey, but I grew up in Kalamazoo. In junior high I was elected "most likely to play shortstop with the _____" (enter the name of the team I do play shortstop with). I was named National High School Player of the Year by the American Baseball Coaches Association in 1992. I received a baseball scholarship to the University of Michigan but was also drafted by Major League Baseball. I went with MLB. I have won several World Series and am currently captain of my team. Who am I?

4. I was born in Mississippi but raised in Dublin, Michigan, by my grandparents. I am an actor. I stuttered as a child, but now my voice is even more famous than my face. Indeed, for my most famous role I act only with my voice. I've won the Tony award twice, first for *The Great White Hope* and then for *Fences*. My first film role was in a movie directed by Stanley Kubrick. I played my most famous role again, many years after my first performance in that role in 1977, but the character is almost two decades younger than he was when I first played him! Who am I?

5. I am a Spring Lake native who is one of the most famous comic strip artists and animators of all time. My most famous creation was a comic strip that featured the narcoleptic adventures of a little boy, which ran in papers between 1905 and 1911. Many comic artists point to it as a seminal influence. My most famous animated cartoon features a mischievous dinosaur; I used to go on vaudeville tours and "interact" with the dinosaur on the screen. I also animated a realistic cartoon about the sinking of the *Lusitania*, with the aim of convincing people that America needed to join World War I. Who am I?

6. I am the youngest person on this list and also the richest, with an estimated personal worth of about 6 billion dollars. I was born in Ann Arbor, and while at Stanford, a buddy and I created a popular Internet application that has become so successful it has become a verb. The company we created around that application has one famous guiding principal in doing business: "Don't be evil." If you've got an Internet connection, chances are very good you've used one of my products recently. Who am I?

For answers, turn to page 307.

MICHIGAN LIGHTHOUSES

- The Livingston Memorial Lighthouse on Belle Isle is the only marble lighthouse in the United States.
- Point Betsie Light was the last manned light on the Great Lakes, until it became automated in 1983.
- Since 1995 Alpena has hosted the Great Lakes Lighthouse Festival, where visitors can tour local lighthouses by air, lake, or land and take part in events designed to stimulate interest and support in the coastal lighthouses. The festival takes place in October.

Hometown:
Land of Sunsets and Stones

*Mother nature must have spent some extra time on this
beautiful town that overlooks Little Traverse Bay.*

Town: Petoskey
Location: Emmet County
Founding: 1896
Current population: 6,200 (est.)
Size: 5 square miles

What's in a Name? The son of a French nobleman and Ottawa
princess, Petosegay (meaning "sunbeams of promise") became
a wealthy fur trader and leader of his tribe. To honor him, in
1873 white settlers named the fledgling town that was growing
up along his land Petoskey, an English adaptation of Petosegay.

Claim to Fame:

- Petoskey stones are fossilized coral that was deposited in the
  area millions of years ago when glaciers moved along the
  bedrock of the Lower Peninsula and plucked up loose
  "stones" along their way. In 1965 the Petoskey stone was

made the official state stone of Michigan. Petoskey stones remain a popular souvenir for visitors, and can still be easily found along the beaches and sand dunes. When polished, they possess a distinctive mottled pattern.

- Nicknamed the "City of the Million-Dollar Sunsets," Petoskey overlooks Little Traverse Bay and its skies often have breathtaking sunsets. The mile-long sandy beach at Petoskey State Park is a popular site for visitors to enjoy the sunsets.

- Millions of passenger pigeons nested in the Petoskey area in the late 1870s; the flocks were so dense that they darkened the skies from morning to evening. But because they were easy to capture and were a known delicacy in many parts of the world, passenger pigeons were targeted by hunters, who caught hundreds at a time with giant nets. Though experts estimate that some 5 billion passenger pigeons once lived on the earth (and made the Great Lakes region their summer home), the species became extinct in 1914 with the death of the last known individual of the species, Martha, in the Cincinnati Zoo.

- Author Ernest Hemingway spent many of his childhood summers vacationing on nearby Walloon Lake. And after being injured in World War I, he recuperated for a winter in a boardinghouse in Petoskey. The town museum, Little Traverse History Museum, has exhibits that detail the time he spent in Petoskey and the surrounding area.

A Banner Unfurled

Here's a primer on the official
flag of the Wolverine state.

Three iterations of the Michigan flag have been created over the years. The first included a portrait of Michigan's first governor, Stevens T. Mason, on one side with the state coat of arms on the other. When the flag was officially adopted in 1865, it was changed to reflect the United States coat of arms on the reverse side. In 1911 the official flag as it is known today was adopted. Only the Michigan coat of arms appears on this flag, on a blue background.

Coat of Arms in Detail

The Michigan coat of arms was adopted at the Constitutional Convention in 1835. General Lewis Cass, a territorial governor, created the design. Like other coats of arms, it represents a mix of national and state symbols.

- The bald eagle, the symbol of the country, represents the authority and jurisdiction of the greater United States over the state of Michigan. The banner above the eagle bears the national motto in Latin, *E pluribus unum,* meaning "From many, one." The arrows, grasped in the talons of the eagle,

symbolize the nation's readiness to defend its principles. The olive branch, with 13 olives, is symbolic of two things: the original 13 colonies and peace.

- The focal point of the arms is the shield, which is supported by an elk and a moose, both native animals to the state. The Latin *Tuebor*, meaning "I will defend" is depicted with the frontiersman on the peninsula. He is sending a double message: a friendly greeting with one hand and a signal of defense (with the rifle) with the other.

- The banner with the Latin phrase, *Si quaeris peninsulam amoenam, circumspice,* translates to "If you seek a pleasant peninsula, look about you." No Michigander needs further explanation of the beauty of the state. Looking around provides all the detail one needs.

The Grand Dame

This hotel, a fixture on Mackinac Island since the late 1800s, is so good, they named it the Grand.

- In 1936 owner W. Stewart Woodfill, looking to spark some publicity, called Robert W. "Believe It or Not" Ripley and told him that the hotel's long-columned porch was 880 feet long. Ripley put the figure in his column and the stat stood for years, until some guys from the *Guinness Book of World Records* showed up in 1981 with surveying equipment and a tape measure. Correction: the porch was 625 feet long. Later expansions now put the much-vaunted veranda at 680 feet.

- The Grand's porch is lined with 2,500 of its signature geraniums in 260 planter boxes. Each fall hotel staffers also plant 25,000 tulips and 15,000 daffodils. Another 125,000 plants are spread throughout the grounds.

- In 1979 *Somewhere in Time*, a time-traveling romantic drama starring Christopher Reeve and Jane Seymour, was filmed at the Grand Hotel. Since then, a longstanding and loyal fan club called the International Network of Somewhere in Time Enthusiasts (INSITE) has hosted a party at the Grand each October. Fans dress in detailed period costumes in tribute to their favorite characters.

- Each of the 385 guest rooms has its own décor and style.

- The swimming pool is named for old-time film star Esther Williams, which is only fitting because *This Time For Keeps*, in which she starred with Jimmy Durante, was shot there.

- Grand Pecan Balls—scoops of ice cream rolled in pecans and topped with fudge sauce—are the hotel's most famous dessert. The staff serves 50,000 of them every year.

- Staying at the Grand means no worries about parking or tipping the valet; cars are not allowed on Mackinac. Visitors from the mainland take a ferry to the island.

- The rule against motorized vehicles extends to the golf course. If players on the Grand's golf course need a lift from the front nine to the back nine, they ride in a horse-drawn golf shuttle.

- Though most of the horses that pull the island carriages belong to a taxi service, the Grand has its own eight-horse stable.

- The Grand has hosted five presidents—Harry S. Truman, John F. Kennedy, Gerald Ford, George Bush, and Bill Clinton—and 23 presidential hopefuls.

- In 1998 the Grand named five rooms after five former First Ladies: Lady Bird Johnson, Betty Ford, Rosalynn Carter, Nancy Reagan, and Barbara Bush.

- When the Grand opens each May, staffers mark the occasion by unrolling a new red carpet down the steps of the famous front porch. The season runs through late October.

Michigan's Lumber Industry

From lumber boom to lumber bust, here's the lowdown on Michigan's big industry of the 1800s.

Before the lumber boom of the mid-1800s, most of Michigan was a densely forested wilderness. (Though Native Americans were the first to fell trees in Michigan, their modest needs had little impact on the forests.) The earliest significant logging in the upper Midwest began with the arrival of the first European settlers. The French built missions, forts, and fur-trading posts out of pine, which was easy to work and grew straight and tall. The largest specimens were 200 feet tall and up to eight feet in diameter. When the British arrived, they used the abundant wood to build their warships and merchant vessels.

The immigrants followed a tradition that had already proved disastrous to the forests of Europe—clear-cutting, a process by which all the trees in a stand of forest are removed. Initially the areas that were clear-cut were relatively small, but as the demand for lumber increased, so did the practice. It wasn't until years later that the effects of deforestation became an issue.

The Sawmill

Commercial lumber production began in earnest in the 1830s, with the appearance of the first sawmills in the Saginaw area. Saginaw was the ideal place for sawmills because it had more than 3 million acres of white pine forests and a network of over 1,500 miles of navigable rivers and streams. (The Saginaw River alone has a total length of 864 miles.) The rivers were crucial to the success of logging because they were the only means of transporting the logs from forest to sawmill.

During the early years, most of the lumber was cut during the winter months because the best way to transport the logs to the rivers was by horse-drawn sleds. The logs were hauled to the banks of the frozen rivers where they were stacked and held until the spring thaw, when they were floated downriver to retention ponds. There, they were sorted and sent to the sawmills for cutting.

Improvement and Innovation

By 1850 the logging industry was expanding rapidly. And by the end of the Civil War, Michigan was the top lumber-producing state in the United States, producing more than 500 million board feet of lumber per year.

Most trees were felled by axes until the 1870s, when cross-cut saws were improved so they could be used to cut down standing timber. Two other innovations during the 1870s made logging a year-round affair—and a very big business. Big Wheels were invented as an alternative to sled transportation. With Big Wheels, logs were suspended from chains attached to the axle of a set of enormous wheels and drawn by a team of horses. And in

1876 the first narrow gauge railroads were built to haul logs, which opened up immense new areas to logging that were previously inaccessible. With a three-foot width, these railroads could transport logs and other materials in terrain that standard railroads couldn't reach. The state granted huge tracts of timberlands to logging companies to get them to improve roads and build new rail lines, and by 1889 at least 89 narrow-gauge railroads were in operation.

The peak of Michigan's great timber harvest was reached between 1889 and 1890, when mills cut a total of 5.5 billion board feet of lumber, most of which was pine.

Measure Once, Cut Twice

Logging companies often did not confine their cutting to the area they had purchased. The common practice of "logging a round forty" meant buying forty acres and then cutting the timber around it far beyond the boundaries to which the title had been secured. By 1900 most of the pine in the Lower Peninsula was gone. In the Upper Peninsula the virgin stands lasted until about 1920.

By the boom's end, logging had stripped 19.5 million acres and left vast tracts of barren wasteland. The lumber barons attempted to unload the now worthless land by using large amounts of fertilizer on "demonstration farms" to convince unsuspecting buyers that the soil was suitable for farming. Some small plots were sold to people who put up their life savings—only to find after a couple of unproductive growing seasons that they had been cheated. But most of the land could not be sold (the lumber barons abandoned it because they did not want to continue paying taxes on it) and it reverted to state ownership.

Repairing Old Damage

During the 1930s, one of the projects assigned to the Civilian Conservation Corps (CCC) was to repair the damage done to the nation's forests by clear-cutting. The CCC planted millions of seedlings and, over time, most of Michigan's barren areas were reforested. However, some areas known as "stump prairies" still exist, even though over a century has passed since they were stripped of trees.

Today over half of Michigan's landmass is covered by forests. Logging, which never disappeared altogether, continues, especially in the state's northern counties. Now, though, it is being done very selectively to preserve and protect the remaining old-growth forests. Tree farming began in 1941 and accounts for the majority of the nearly 675 million board feet of lumber that Michigan produces annually. Michigan also produces over 15 million Christmas trees each year, representing approximately 15 percent of the nation's supply.

DID YOU KNOW?

The Tahquamenon Logging Museum and Nature Study near Newbury preserves original buildings, equipment, and memorabilia from the logging era, including an authentic cook shack, an original CCC building, and a family dwelling. A boardwalk allows visitors to follow a nature trail adjacent to the Tahquamenon River and Forest.

No Kiddie Without a Christmas

*With the help of the Detroit Goodfellows,
needy Detroit children have had their Christmas
wishes come true for nearly a century.*

In 1914 successful Detroit businessman James Brady was inspired by a *Detroit News* cartoon that showed a man balancing a stack of Christmas gifts with one arm and holding the hand of a small, disheveled newsboy with the other. Reminded of his childhood days spent hawking newspapers on the streets after his father died, Brady realized he could help the less fortunate kids of Detroit—whose lives were so similar to his own childhood—have a brighter Christmas.

Back to the Streets

Enlisting the help of the Detroit Newsboys Association for a few days that December, Brady and more than 70 "Old Newsboys" once again returned to the streets, this time to hawk special holiday edition newspapers. Proceeds from the paper sales came to a little over $2,000 that first year, and gifts were delivered to the homes of needy children on Christmas morning.

"Papes!"

Ninety plus years later, the fundraiser has grown into a million-dollar annual effort carried out much the same way it began. Except now it has expanded to some 300 volunteers—former newsboys and girls, known as "Detroit Goodfellows," as well as policemen and firemen—who hawk "Goodfellow Editions" of the *Detroit News* and the *Detroit Free Press* on the street corners of Detroit. The price of a paper is "anything you care to pay."

Because the Old Newsboys members pick up the administrative costs of the fundraiser, all the proceeds go to the kids' Christmas presents. Of the current generation of Goodfellows, many are happy to acknowledge being recipients of the Goodfellow boxes themselves as children. "In my neighborhood, the only time you were happy to see a cop at the door was on Christmas Eve!" said one Goodfellow.

What's in a Box?

The annual fundraiser benefits needy Detroit-area children between the ages of five and 13. The kids not only get Christmas packages filled with warm clothes, shoes, candy, and toys, but they also receive dental care and other benefits that continue throughout the year.

A monument was erected on Central Avenue, between Williams and Scott, in Brady's honor following his death in 1928. Next time you walk by it in December, be sure to buy a paper from a Goodfellow.

Top Pop

*Al Kaline, The Temptations, and the Ford Mustang are not the
only classics that Michigan can lay claim to. Vernor's Ginger Ale—the
nation's oldest soda pop—has been produced in Michigan since 1866.
Vernor's was heralded a classic long before the '68 series, the debut of
Motown, or Detroit Muscle made its introduction on Woodward Avenue.
Michiganders proudly hail Vernor's as their unofficial state pop.*

James Vernor was working as a 15-year-old errand boy at a
Detroit drugstore. Intrigued by one of the store's products,
an amber ginger ale imported from Ireland, he set to work on
his own ginger concoction in 1862. Shortly thereafter, Vernor
abandoned his experimentation to enlist with the Union Army's
Fourth Michigan Cavalry. He left behind his mix of ginger,
vanilla, and 17 other special ingredients in an oak barrel. Upon
his return four years later, he opened his own drug store at 235
Woodward Avenue. He also was pleased to discover that his
barrel of ginger ale had aged to perfection in his absence.

Vernor made more of the ginger ale and served it in his
drugstore's soda fountain for the next 30 years. It wasn't exactly
an overnight sensation, but it eventually became so popular
that Vernor sold his beverage in other regions, including
Buffalo, Toledo, Cleveland, and Niagara Falls. Vernor was a

stickler for maintaining consistent taste and quality for his ginger ale and his emphasis on quality contributed to his success and a growing loyal clientele. Demand skyrocketed.

Hitting the Big Time

Ginger ale was the top soda pop for decades and Vernor's had numerous competitors, but Prohibition contributed to the beverage's decline in popularity. Ginger ale's association with alcohol as a popular mixer for cocktails caused the many new teetotalers to abandon the beverage. Vernor's, with its rich golden color and distinctive taste and bite, remained popular in Michigan and some other areas, but is not a nationally known brand like Canada Dry's ginger ale.

In 1966 a group of investors purchased the company and later sold it to A&W in 1987, who then sold it to Cadbury Schweppes in 1993. The recipe was not altered, and Cadbury Schweppes owns and produces Vernor's to this day. For this, Michiganders heave a sigh of relief. It wouldn't be Michigan without Vernor's Ginger Ale.

DID YOU KNOW?

Michigan was the first state in the nation to enact a "bottle bill." In 1976 the new law required a ten-cent deposit for recyclable soft drink and alcoholic beverage containers, spawning a new industry in recycling.

Hometown:
Gateway to the U.P.

*This scenic burg is home to one of the world's biggest
machines and is a haven for Yoopers and tourists alike.*

Town: Iron Mountain
Location: Dickinson County
Founding: 1879
Current population: 8,100 (est.)
Size: 7.2 square miles

What's in a Name?

When iron deposits were discovered in the 1870s, early settlers
who came for the lumber began mining iron instead. When the
town was founded a few years later, nothing was better suited to
the town name than the industry it was now known for.

Claim to Fame:

- Iron Mountain's Pine Mountain Ski Jump is one of the
  world's tallest artificial ski jumps. It boasts a ten-story scaf-
  fold, a 381-foot slide, and a 349-foot landing hill. Estimated
  takeoff speeds are 55 to 60 mph, and landing speeds are

roughly 65 mph. The jump was built in the 1930s and hosts an annual competition each February. Many records have been set on the jump, including an international mark of 459 feet, which was established by two skiers: Japan's Masahiko Harada in 1996, and Finland's Kalle Keituri in 2002.

- Each winter, roughly 35,000 to 50,000 hibernating bats occupy the mine shaft at Iron Mountain's abandoned Millie Hill mine, which has a year-round temperature of about 45° F. In 1992 the mine was scheduled to be backfilled with tons of dirt, but the bats' winter shelter was spared after it was determined to be one of the most important bat sites in the country. A special steel cage was installed at the top of the mine's 300-foot vertical shaft. Its unique design allows the mine to be safely sealed while bats come and go as they please.

- Iron Mountain is credited with being the birthplace of the ubiquitous pillow-shaped briquette known as Kingsford Charcoal. In the early 1900s, Henry Ford operated a sawmill in the woods surrounding Iron Mountain where parts for the Ford "Woody" automobile line were produced. Ever inventive, Ford followed a method that transformed sawdust into the famous charcoal briquette. A fully operational charcoal plant was born in 1921 and was managed by E.G. Kingsford, a lumberman and distant relative of Ford.

- Three miles east of town, the House of Yesteryear has over 30 vintage automobiles on display from the early 20th century, as well as vintage vacuum cleaners, a foot-operated dentist's drill, 150-year-old farm implements, and a dog-powered washing machine.

- The Cornish Pump is the largest steam engine ever built in North America. It was designed to keep water out of the old Chapin iron mine, which was rumored to be the "wettest mine in the world." The 160-ton crimson behemoth has a 40-foot flywheel, stands 54 feet tall, and is housed in the Cornish Pumping Engine and Mining Museum and Gift Shop. The museum also contains one of the largest collections of underground mining equipment in the state, as well as other oddities such as a folding oak bathtub, an American and European late-19th century doll collection, and an 8.5-foot World War II CG4A glider replica.

- Guided underground train tours are offered at the Iron Mountain Iron Mine, which was functional for 68 years and mined 21.6 million tons of iron ore in its nearly seven decades of existence. The big stope—or mined-out area beneath the earth's surface—is 630 feet long, 400 feet wide, and 200 feet high.

"FRESH AS DEW FROM KALAMAZOO"

Early Dutch pioneers in Kalamazoo cleverly converted the area's marshlands into celery fields. From the 1890s to the 1930s, Kalamazoo shipped celery all over the country and was known as the "Celery Capital of the World." Nowadays, visitors can revisit those halcyon days at the Celery Flats Interpretive Center, which has displays, artifacts, a celery field, and personal recollections of the celery farmers.

A Fun Run

In 1994 Trenary resident Toivo Aho heard about an outhouse race
in another state. He and his friends and neighbors thought that it
would be a great way to pass the time during the long winter. Little
did they know that they had given birth to a new Michigan tradition.

Because of Aho's brainstorm, on the last Saturday in
February in Trenary, Michigan, you can see a most unusual
sight: people pushing outhouses on skis down Main Street. It
could be to beat cabin fever—the area averages 120–140 inches
of snow a year. Or it could be for the cash prizes totaling more
than $1,000. Whatever the case, the rules are simple: 1) Build
an outhouse with wood, cardboard, etc. 2) Put in a toilet seat
and a roll of toilet paper. (An *Uncle John's Bathroom Reader*
would be a nice touch.) 3) Mount it on skis. 4) Pick a partner
and push it as fast as you can for about 500 feet. The three
fastest outhouses win.

By 2005 the race had celebrated its 12th anniversary.
Recent races have all been built around themes: Let's Potty at
the Dozenth Ever Trenary Outhouse Classic, Leap into the 11th
Ever Outhouse Classic, Get Privy to Da 8th Wonder of the
World, and more.

And it's not just small-town fun—the races have developed
a national cult following. In this town of less than 1,000

people, the number of onlookers swells to more than 4,500 on race day, by some estimates. In 2005 there were even race entries from New York, Indiana, and Wisconsin.

Toilet Humor

Each year there also seems to be some form of a public privy. Sometimes the back wall is missing or the walls are see-through. To convert it to a private privy, builders usually advise would-be users to close their eyes. Politics aren't off-limits either. One year a participant brought a "Forty Million Dollar Inaugural Pottie" (aka the Oval Office). The White House–shaped outhouse came stocked with $100 bill–printed toilet paper that was dubbed "taxpayer money."

Once the races are done, there's also snow volleyball, plenty of food, and a chance to shop for one-of-a-kind gifts and souvenirs: official Outhouse Classic shirts, sweatshirts, caps, and headbands. If you're looking for something to do at the end of February, the organizers say there's always room for one more—as long as you are not a party pooper.

DID YOU KNOW?

One of the last remaining two-story outhouses in the United States is in Cedar Lake. William Nelson built the outhouse next to his general store nearly 100 years ago. Although there have been several attempts to move it to a nearby museum, the two-story outhouse is currently on private property.

Tales of the Third Coast

*Looking for something good to read? Here's some of
Uncle John's favorite books set in the Wolverine State.*

Them, Joyce Carol Oates

Them concentrates thematically on class, race, and urban life in
Detroit during the years between 1937 and 1967, via Loretta
Wendall and her children Maureen and Jules. It's often cited as
Joyce Carol Oates's finest novel. The Maureen Wendall charac-
ter is based on one of Oates's own students at the University of
Detroit, where the author taught English from 1962 to 1967.
Oates defines the book as a work of "history in fictional form,"
and her emotionally exhausting tale won the 1970 National
Book Award for fiction.

Song of Solomon, Toni Morrison

Song of Solomon put Toni Morrison "on the map," as they say,
bringing her a great deal of critical acclaim and commercial
success. The book follows the saga of Macon "Milkman" Dead,
a child born into a dysfunctional African American family in
northern Michigan. Macon is eventually led down a path of
self-discovery (one that parallels an African American folktale
wherein slaves fly back to Africa), and his story is filled with

Morrison's graceful prose. Said prose has been described as stunningly beautiful by many critics—even when it happens to intertwine with brutally violent imagery and overtly sexual content. Oprah Winfrey's book club has given *Song of Solomon* invaluable amounts of publicity over the years.

The Tarnished Eye, Judith Guest

The Tarnished Eye is based on real-life murders that transpired in Michigan during the 1960s. Set in the fictional northern Michigan community of Blessed, the novel takes us into the mind of Sheriff Hugh DeWitt, who must solve the brutal murder of a family of six. Eventually, he is led to Ann Arbor, where he finds a new set of murders, notable for their resemblance to the carnage in Blessed.

Anatomy of a Murder, Robert Traver

Robert Traver—a pen name for Ispheming native John D. Voelker—was sitting on the Michigan State Supreme Court bench when his novel was published in 1958. The book was largely based on the 1952 Big Bay Lumberjack Tavern murder trial, in which Voelker was the defense attorney, and it quickly became a best seller in the United States. Voelker represented a U.S. Army officer who was on trial for murdering a Big Bay bartender in an alleged act of vengeance. The court was reportedly in such a hurry to get the trial underway that the last juror chosen was not even asked if he knew the deceased (he did). Hollywood glitzed up the book with a film adaptation starring Jimmy Stewart, released in 1959.

52 Pickup, Elmore Leonard

Bloomfield Hills resident Elmore Leonard's first Detroit novel—from 1974—involves a kidnapping, $52,000 dollars, and a booby-trapped briefcase. Detroit businessman Harry Mitchell gets caught on film cheating on his wife (at a strip club, no less), and he finds himself embroiled in a blackmail caper. Harry's blackmailers get more than they bargained for, though, as the former combat veteran proves to be a formidable foe—one quite capable of outwitting his nemeses. Plot twists abound in *52 Pickup*, and Harry engages in an entertaining cat-and-mouse game with the villains. Leonard went on to set most of his books in the vicinity of Detroit.

Motor City Blue, Loren D. Estleman

The first of the hard-boiled, Amos Walker detective series, *Blue* has Marlowe-esque private detective Amos Walker hunting down a missing teenage mob ward named Marla Bernstein. Walker's only clue to Bernstein's whereabouts is a pornographic photo of the girl that leads him into the seamy underworld of Detroit's smut culture. Estleman animates the hard-drinking Walker with slow-moving prose that is set against an effective noir backdrop, and the trail—or lack thereof—left by Bernstein gets dirtier and more baffling with each twist and turn. Consider *Motor City Blue* recommended reading if you are a Raymond Chandler buff (and even if you are not).

Poets of the Third Coast

Many poets have contributed to Michigan's literary history. Here are a few of the best:

- **Diane Wakoski.** Wakoski has published over 50 books of poetry and is best known for a collection called *The Leather Jacket Diaries.* Her early work was part of the "deep image" movement of Robert Kelly, Jerome Rothenberg, and others. She teaches creative writing at Michigan State University and continues to be a treasured and significant literary presence.

- **Edgar Guest.** Judith Guest's great uncle's work was popular in the first half of the 20th century. His career started at the *Detroit Free Press.* While working there as a reporter, Guest started writing daily poems that were syndicated in newspapers throughout the country. *Reader's Digest* aficionados will notice that his work sometimes still appears there.

- **Theodore Roethke.** The Saginaw-born Theodore Roethke was awarded the Pulitzer Prize in 1953 for his book *The Waking.* His lyrical pieces were dominated by natural themes and images. Roethke went on to have a significant presence in the Pacific Northwest (he died in Bainbridge Island, Washington, but he was laid to rest in Saginaw).

- **Robert Hayden.** Hayden, an African American, was elected to the American Academy of Poets in 1975. His best-known work is "The Whipping," a poem that poignantly examines child abuse.

- **Henry Wadsworth Longfellow.** Although he was born in Maine, Longfellow's popular epic, *Song of Hiawatha,* was set on the Upper Peninsula shore of Lake Superior. An important piece of literature, *Hiawatha* drew most of its inspiration from the stories of the Ojibway tribe and the writings of explorer Henry Rowe Schoolcraft.

It's Beautiful to Be Belgian

*Detroit's Cadieux Café is a living legend. Hipsters
old and new fill its tables and try their hand at
the café's signature sport: feather bowling.*

Boston may have its Bull and Finch, but metro Detroit has
its own claim to fame: the Cadieux Café, the only place in
the United States where you can play a bizarre yet oddly satis-
fying game known as feather bowling. Pronounced KADGE-
you, the little brown brick building on Cadieux Road opened
just after Prohibition ended. It started as a social club inside a
neighborhood populated with Belgian immigrants.

In the Cadieux Café, recent immigrants could live like they
did in the old country, cursing in Flemish, drinking favorite
brews, and throwing wooden wheels down dirt lanes toward
pigeon feathers. Ah, did we mention the brews? Of 70 beers
served, 22 are Belgian with names like Corsendonk, Chimay
Grand Reserve, and Liefmans Goudenband.

Hit the Lanes

The Cadieux retains its original charm with dim lighting, a bar
at one end that seats about a dozen, and a café filled with long
tables that force strangers to become friends. Oval portraits of
the café's founders stare down at new generations of guests.

The main draw is the Belgian game of feather bowling. Think of it as a mix of horseshoes and boccie ball. The two lanes, a mixture of kitty litter, peat, and dirt enriched with ox blood, are separated by a thin strip of AstroTurf. The lanes are located through a door off the restaurant and they're rarely empty.

The original lane, built in 1931, was outside. A second was built two years later, and the area was enclosed in 1939. Current owner Ron Devos opened them to the public in 1977, and the Cadieux has been rolling ever since. The balls resemble cheese wheels, said to be the choice of the game's cheese-making founders. They weigh about five pounds each and are bent from years of pounding the concave lanes.

A Fine Feather

The goal of the game is to roll the balls toward a pigeon feather that sticks up out of the dirt at the end of the lane. The feathers are about 60 feet apart. The team that gets ten points first wins. Sounds easy, but it's not. The lanes are bumpy, and the balls are dented. But landing one near the coveted feather is a glorious achievement.

Today's players missed the bar's more exciting days when archery and pigeon racing also graced the Cadieux. Imagine trying that when you've got a few of those Liefmans in your gullet.

Thursday is league night; otherwise, the lanes are open to the public. But call ahead—weekend nights are booked months in advance.

UM vs. OSU

ESPN ranked this annual sporting event the greatest rivalry of all sports, giving bragging rights to the winners and excuses for the losers.

Even though the University of Michigan and Ohio State University are separated by less than 200 miles, they might as well be light-years apart in their feelings toward each other. So what makes a rivalry? Two teams wanting the same goal. Throw in some colorful personalities, a close distance, and some healthy animosity, and let simmer over 100 years. That's the UM vs. OSU recipe for a great rivalry, best served over conference titles and bowl games.

The Games

The first game of this incredible rivalry started in 1897 in Ann Arbor. The University of Michigan walloped Ohio State University 34–0. In fact OSU didn't beat the Wolverines until well into the next century when in 1919 they won 13–3. The first time both teams were in the Big Ten Conference was in 1918.

The tradition of saving the best for last did not start until 1935. Since then the UM vs. OSU game has been the last game on their schedules. Frequently, this game is the most decisive.

UM and OSU have faced off 20 times since 1935 to decide the winner of the Big Ten and the team to play in the Rose Bowl.

Bo Knows Woody

The greatest coaching rivalry between these teams was fought by Wayne Woodrow Hayes, known as "Woody," and Glenn "Bo" Schembechler. Bo actually played for Woody at Miami University of Ohio. The Big Ten conference under their regimes became known as the Big Two and Little Eight as UM and OSU so dominated the conference from 1969 to 1978. In fact, legend has it that Woody could not even utter the name Michigan University; instead he called the school the "school up north." When Woody had to venture to the "school up north," he made sure his gas tank was full. He refused to spend even a dime in Michigan, so once, when his car ran out of gas a few miles away from the Ohio border, he pushed his car back into Ohio. Bo won the rivalry slightly, compiling a 5–4–1 record. Both were national coach of the year: Woody in 1968 and 1979, and Bo in 1969.

Eight Big-Ten Games For the Books

- **1897** At the first meeting of UM vs. OSU, UM won by a shutout of 34–0.

- **1922** Ohio Stadium opened and UM played the role of spoiler by winning 19–0 in Ohio's own yard.

- **1927** Michigan Stadium opened and UM defeated OSU during the dedication game 24–0.

- **1940** UM won 40–0 in Ohio under the leadership of Tom Harmon, who ran for two touchdowns, passed for two more, and returned an interception for a touchdown.

- **1950** Best known as the "Snow Bowl," both teams combined for 45 punts in the middle of a snowstorm. UM went on to upset OSU with a 9–3 victory, spoiling OSU's Big Ten title chance.

- **1968** OSU defeated UM 50–14 and went on to win the Big Ten and the Rose Bowl.

- **1969** UM handed number-one ranked OSU a 24–12 loss. As a result, both teams shared the Big Ten championship and UM got a ticket to the Rose Bowl.

- **1973** A 10–10 tie resulted in both teams sharing the Big Ten title. Athletic directors voted to send OSU to the Rose Bowl.

Who Flipped My Car? During the 1980s football season, if you were a student at UM but drove a car with Ohio license plates, you had to get a special sticker for your car so overzealous fans wouldn't turn over your car.

Love Can Wait. A father told his daughter he would pay for her entire wedding so long as the wedding did not fall on the day of the UM/OSU game. Of course, the church and reception hall were only available on game day. The father regretfully informed his daughter he would not be in attendance at her wedding. The daughter ended up postponing the wedding for six months.

You Paid What? Tickets for the UM/OSU matchup are so in demand that a pair of $100 tickets will quickly sell for $400 and can even fetch up to $900.

We Get Letters

*Neither rain, nor sleet, nor 15-foot waves
can keep the J. W. Wescott II down. Find out
more about Michigan's floating post office!*

How do sailors get their mail while at sea? For vessels passing through Detroit, the answer is simple: it's "mail-by-the-pail," courtesy of the *J. W. Wescott II*. Built in 1949 and refitted in 1992, the *J. W. Wescott II* is a 45-foot, single-propeller ship that the U.S. Postal Service contracted to deliver mail to ships while they are underway. The *Westcott's* unique and highly valued service makes Detroit the only place in the United States where ships can mail documents and receive deliveries without pulling into port.

Out in a Boat

Owned and operated by the J. W. Wescott Company, the diesel-powered boat can reach a top cruising speed of 15 knots, making mail delivery quick and highly efficient. Mind you, that wasn't always the case. J. W. Wescott himself began his service in 1874 using only a rowboat to greet incoming vessels. Back then his job was to inform ships of changing orders. It wasn't until 21 years later in June 1895 that he completed his first midriver mail delivery. These days the *J. W. Westcott II*'s services have expanded to include mail and freight delivery, storage, passenger and pilot boat services, laundry, and the sale of nautical charts and sundries. The boat has even been known to deliver pizza to grateful sailors. Once a year the *J. W. Westcott II* also enters the Detroit River International Freedom Festival tugboat races.

Shipshape and Ready to Deliver

So just how does the *J. W. Westcott II* get its job done? Mail is delivered to the J. W. Westcott company office via the United States Postal Service every day. It's then sorted according to vessel name and placed into the appropriate mailbox. When that boat passes through the Detroit River system, its mail is delivered by the *J. W. Wescott II*, along with any supplies it may have requested in advance.

When the ship is only a few hundred yards away, the *J. W. Wescott II* slides into action, nestling beside the larger vessel midship, while its crew lowers an oversized bucket to collect all incoming mail. Timing is of the essence, as the *Wescott* must match the other vessel's speed. Fortunately, the act is made easier through one of the *Westcott*'s special features: a clear Plexiglas roof above the pilothouse that allows the helmsman to stay in visual contact with the deckhands at all times. The *J. W. Westcott II* then returns to port, ready to repeat this same routine as many as 60 times a day, each and every day during the navigation season. Along the way, they'll battle rough moorings, choppy seas, and imposing currents. But at least they don't have to contend with hungry dogs.

Pass the Turkey

*It's not turkey day without a Detroit Lions game. The
tradition began in 1934, when the Lions joined the NFL, and
it shows no sign of stopping. Here's how it all got started.*

When the Portsmouth (Ohio) Spartans of the young
National Football League were put up for sale in 1934,
George A. Richards, owner of radio station WJR, and his part-
ners paid $7,952.08 for the franchise and moved it to Detroit.
Richards, who knew a thing or two about promotions, decided
his new team needed to have a claim to fame. And a
Thanksgiving game would be just the ticket.

Game of the Year

Richards rescheduled the Sunday game between the Lions and
the Chicago Bears for Thanksgiving Day. Coming into the
game, the Lions had a strong 10–1 record, but that only gave
them second place, behind the Bears, who were 11–0. The
matchup was so attractive that NBC arranged to cover the
game on radio on over 90 stations, making it the first NFL
game to be nationally broadcast. More than 26,000 fans
watched the game at the University of Detroit stadium—twice
the Lions' normal crowd—and thousands more were turned

away. Although the game was a success on the airwaves and in the stands, on the field the Lions lost to the Bears, 19–16. Still, a tradition was born. More than six decades later, football rivals turkey as a Thanksgiving staple in Detroit and throughout the country. The Detroit Thanksgiving Day game is a league tradition. The Lions are always scheduled for a home game on that date, and the game is always broadcast nationally.

Detroit Lions By the Numbers

11/29/34: The Lions hosted their first Thanksgiving Day game in their first year in the National Football League. The home team lost to the Chicago Bears, 19–16.

1956: First year the Thanksgiving Day game was televised.

2002: First year the Lions played their annual Thanksgiving game at their new home, Ford Field.

65: Number of Thanksgiving Day games the Lions have played through the 2004 season.

33–30–2: Lions' overall record on Thanksgiving, through the 2004 season.

3.5 million: Total number of fans who have attended Lions' Thanksgiving Day games throughout the years.

12–0: Lowest scoring game in Lions' Thanksgiving Day history—the Philadelphia Eagles beat Detroit by that score in 1968.

273: Number of rushing yards gained by the Buffalo Bills' O. J. Simpson against the Lions on Thanksgiving Day 1976. It was the league's single-game rushing record at the time, but the Lions won the game, 27–14.

17: Number of times the Lions have played the Green Bay Packers on Thanksgiving, through 2004. It was the most appearances in the holiday game by any Lions opponent.

11–5–1: The Lions' Thanksgiving record against the Packers, through 2004.

11: Number of times the Lions sacked Bart Starr on Thanksgiving 1962. By beating the Packers 26–14, the Lions ended Green Bay's ten-game winning streak.

4: Number of stadiums where the Lions have played Thanksgiving Day games—University of Detroit Stadium from 1934 to 1937, Briggs Stadium/Tiger Stadium from 1938 to 1974, the Silverdome from 1975 to 2001, and Ford Field from 2002 on.

DID YOU KNOW?

In 1936, in Nazi-run Berlin, UM senior Sam Stoller made Olympic history by not playing. Stoller was dropped from the 400-meter relay on the morning of the preliminary heats. There were immediate protests that track coach Lawrence Robinson and Avery Brundage, president of the U.S. Olympics committee, had dropped Stoller (along with his Jewish teammate Mary Glickman) to avoid offending their anti-Semitic Nazi hosts. Stoller and Glickman were the only Jewish members on the U.S. track team and the only ones ordered not to participate.

Hometown:
Anatomy of a Village

This town has it all: international intrigue, monsters, and even large quantities of Olympic athletes in residence.

Town: Marquette
Location: Marquette County
Founding: 1871
Current population: 20,500 (est.)
Size: 11.4 square miles

What's in a Name?

This small town was originally named Worcester, after the Worcester in Massachusetts. The name was later changed to Marquette, in honor of Father Jacques Marquette, a great French explorer of the area.

Claim to Fame:

- Designated a Strategic Air Command Base during the Cold War, the K. I. Sawyer Air Force Base outside Marquette was a top-ten target for Russia. It kept a Stealth Bomber in its hangars during the early 1990s.

- Young Olympic athletes study in the country's only United States Olympic Education Center at Northern Michigan University. If the athletes aren't yet college age, they attend high school classes at Marquette High.

- Many scenes from the 1959 movie *Anatomy of a Murder* starring Jimmy Stewart were filmed in Marquette, primarily in the county courthouse. The film dramatized a well-known murder that occurred in the area. See "Tales of the Third Coast" on page 250.

- The Marquette area is home to the legendary Marquette Monster. Described by Father Jacques Marquette in 1673 during his travels along the Mississippi, the monster's "head was like that of a tiger, his nose was sharp, and somewhat resembled a wildcat, his beard was long, his ears stood upright, the color of his head was gray, and his neck was black." It is similar to the Piasa Monster Bird.

- Built in 1991 for Northern Michigan University, the Yooper Dome is the world's largest wooden dome. It is supported by some 701 fir beams. The dome is primarily used for athletic events.

- The town is an important Lake Superior port for iron ore and lumber.

DID YOU KNOW?

Michigan claims to have more tree varieties than all of Europe.

"One Day, Eino and Toivo . . ."

Enjoy the exploits of the Upper Peninsula's own dynamic duo.

Eino and Toivo are the heroes of Yooper lore, a couple of local everymen who have been memorialized in jokes and anecdotes. Most Eino and Toivo jokes begin with the pair either hunting or fishing (two favorite Yooper pastimes) while hanging out in prominent U.P. locales, drinking beer and enjoying life.

Eino and Toivo reflect the deep Finnish roots prevalent across Michigan's Upper Peninsula. Originally viewed as Finnish stereotypes, they have since become a part of local pride and regional recognition. They may be a bit slow, but their adventures are on the tongues of nearly every Michigan resident north of the Mackinac Bridge.

* * *

Eino and Toivo found work with the County Highway Commission to paint new road lines along the 35 out of Escanaba. The first day out, they managed to paint ten full miles of road. Their boss was so impressed, he gave them both a raise. The second day, they painted only two miles. The boss was disappointed, but decided to let it slide. The third day, Eino and Toivo only painted 500 feet of road! This, the boss couldn't let slide. He called Eino and Toivo into his office the next day and demanded an explanation.

"Geez, boss," Eino said, "We can't help it! Every day we get farther away from the paint can!"

* * *

One day, Eino and Toivo went hunting in the woods north of Ishpeming, and they decided to split up to cover more ground. "Okay, Toivo," Eino said, "I'll go left, an' you go right. If you get lost, just fire three shots into the air, an' I'll come find you." Toivo agreed, and they went their separate ways. After a few hours, Toivo realized that he was lost. He aimed his weapon into the air, fired off three shots, and prayed, "Please God, let Eino see my arrows!"

* * *

Eino and Toivo were headed out to deer camp for the first day of the hunting season. They stopped for supplies on the way, and while Toivo gassed up the truck, Eino bought some pasties to eat on the drive up. When he got back to the truck, Toivo saw the pasty bag and said, "Hey, Eino, if I can guess how many pasties are in that bag, will you give me one of 'em?"

"Toivo," Eino replied, "if you can guess how many pasties are in this bag, I'll give you both of 'em!"

"Holywha? Okay, then . . . I think you got five."

* * *

Eino and Toivo were headed to Michigammee, and for once Toivo was driving. When they reached the traffic light in

Negaunee, the light was red. Toivo drove straight through it without slowing. "Holywha!" Eino cried. "Toivo, what're ya doin' runnin' da red light?"

Toivo replied, "Don't worry. My brudder taught me how to drive."

Soon they reached the light in Ishpeming, which was red. Toivo drove straight through it. "Toivo, why do you keep runnin' dem red lights?" Eino asked.

"Don't worry," Toivo insisted. "My brudder taught me how to drive."

When they got to the light in West Ishpeming, Eino was relieved to see that the light was green. But suddenly, Toivo slammed on the brakes and screeched to a halt. "Toivo," Eino screamed, "what're ya doin' now?"

Toivo replied, "Well, my brudder might be comin' da other way."

DID YOU KNOW?

- "Eino" means "lone warrior" in Finnish; "Toivo" means "hope."

- Eino and Toivo have lent their names to a brand of pasty sauce.

- Eino and Toivo are popular subjects for Da Yoopers, the Michigan sketch comedy group best known for their song, "The Second Week of Deer Camp."

- Minnesotans have their own version of Eino and Toivo—two Norwegian pals named Sven and Oli.

Spilling His Guts

Some of the biggest scientific breakthroughs
have come about by accident. Here's one story of
doctoral ingenuity from Plunges Into the Universe.

D r. William Beaumont was a frustrated army surgeon. Stationed on Mackinac Island in Lake Huron as part of a peacekeeping force in 1822, he felt that his surgical skills were being wasted. With nothing to interrupt the tranquility of the island, Beaumont had little call for his talents. That was until one day when a drunken man accidentally discharged his rifle into the torso of a fur trader by the name of Alexis St. Martin.

Tummy Tribulations

Beaumont rushed to the young man's side to find a massive hole where his belly button had been. Part of the stomach was actually spilling out. Expecting the man to die, Beaumont cleaned the wound and applied a dressing. St. Martin did not die. Instead his stomach healed in a very strange way—the stomach attached itself to the wall of his chest, while the hole remained open so people could see inside the man's stomach.

One Giant Leap for Digestion Studies

Dr. Beaumont immediately recognized the opportunity this presented. He could be the first man to study and examine a living digestive system. Convincing St. Martin to cooperate, Beaumont began experimenting by tying tiny bits of food on silk threads and inserting them in St. Martin's stomach. Periodically he would remove them to observe the state of digestion. Such experiments continued for a dozen years, leading to a new branch of science—the study of human digestion—and making celebrities of both Beaumont and St. Martin (whose tummy window stayed open for the rest of his life).

DID YOU KNOW?

Based on tornado data collected from 1950 to 2001, the place in Michigan where you are most likely to be hit by a tornado is the area roughly 20 miles east of Hillsdale on Interstate 127 between the cities of Addison and Hudson. The effects of 44 tornados have passed through or within 20 miles of this point.

On June 8, 1953, the first of only two F5 tornados ever to hit Michigan wreaked havoc across Ohio and Ontario, Canada, before settling in Michigan. According to the Fujita Scale, which ranks tornado intensity, an F5 tornado is the most destructive funnel.

The "Beecher Tornado" did the greatest damage along a four-mile stretch of Coldwater Road where 113 people were killed. This tornado spawned eight smaller tornados that caused much of the 925 injuries and $19 million in damage. In total, 340 homes were destroyed and over 250 were damaged.

B-24s:
Built for the Road Ahead

*The United States produced over 300,000 aircraft
in World War II, and a good chunk of them
were built in Willow Run, Michigan.*

W hen Nazi Germany began bombing England in 1940,
the American government began to gear up war production, including rapid production of the strategic B-24
"Liberator" bomber. The U.S. Army Air Force feared that San
Diego's Consolidated Aircraft Corporation, the B-24's designer,
lacked the facilities to build the bomber in sufficient quantities.
Instead, the production contract went to one of America's
largest manufacturers and the birthplace of the assembly line.
Ford Motor Company was awarded the B-24 contract despite
concerns that an automotive company would prove unable to
switch to aircraft production.

How to Build an Aircraft Plant in Six Months—Sort Of
Henry Ford picked a site near Ann Arbor, Michigan, to build
the B-24 plant. A nearby creek called Willow Run lent its name
to the plant, which was nicknamed "the Run." Originally envisioned as a single colossal assembly line, Ford realized that a

mile-long building would run out of conservative Washtenaw County and into more liberal, unionized Wayne County, and therefore he changed the design to an inefficient L-shape. When production began on May 14, 1942, the Run was 67 acres large, the single biggest industrial structure in the world. Charles Lindbergh called it "the Grand Canyon of the mechanized world." It would employ over 40,000 workers, including "little people" brought to work in the B-24's tiny wing spaces.

Arsenal of Democracy

After the Japanese attack on Pearl Harbor on December 7, 1941, war production took on a new urgency. Plans called for Willow Run to produce one B-24 bomber an hour. The American public, disheartened by Japanese victories in the Pacific and the German dominance of Europe, latched onto Willow Run as a symbol of hope, part of the "Arsenal of Democracy" that would defeat the Axis powers. The *Detroit Free Press* exulted that the plant was "a promise of revenge for Pearl Harbor. You know when you see Willow Run that in the end we will give it to them good." Writer Westbrook Pegler called it "the damnedest colossus the industrial world has ever seen."

Turbulence Ahead

The Run faced enormous difficulties getting off the ground. It was a stupendous amount of work for an automotive company to learn to build bombers, and numerous practical problems plagued production. Most of the Run's workers lived in Detroit, a two-hour commute away. Gasoline, rationed for the military's tanks and trucks, was costly and ate up most of the workers' wages. The company considered building onsite housing, but Henry Ford proved hostile to the idea. Consequently, absenteeism often ran from 10 to 15 percent. In addition, the B-24 went through over 500 design modifications during the war, each one a tremendous logistical change requiring a substantial change in the plant's machinery, training, personnel, and line operations.

Despite the fanfare of the plant's first year, Willow Run's nagging problems persisted. All of these difficulties added up to an abysmal first year for the plant. By September 1942, after four months of production, Willow Run had produced exactly two bombers—one of them nothing more than spare parts, packed in crates. Willow Run became a national disgrace just as quickly as it had become a patriotic symbol and picked up the nickname "Will It Run?" The Senate launched an investigation into the plant's poor performance in 1943, and the government considered pushing out Ford Motor Company and taking control of the plant itself.

Practice Makes Perfect

But things turned around for Willow Run. Constant practice, increased experience, and the demands of wartime gradually ironed out the production difficulties. Eventually dormitory-style housing was raised to accommodate workers, but in the interim a new highway was built specifically for Willow Run, and Michigan Central ran a train line to the plant to help commuting workers.

These improvements bore fruit. By 1944 the Run was producing one B-24 every 63 minutes. By the end of the war, the

Run had churned out 8,685 B-24 bombers, the U.S. Army Air Force's main bomber in Europe. After a rocky start, the men and women of the plant had indeed made Willow Run one of the arsenals of democracy. As Walter Reuther said, "America's [battles] were won on the assembly lines of Detroit."

DID YOU KNOW?

"Rosie the Riveter," a symbol of women's contribution to factory work in World War II, first appeared in the 1942 song, "Rosie the Riveter," by Kay Kyser. When the government needed a real-life Rosie to participate in a film promoting the war effort, they found their star at Willow Run: Rose Will Monroe, a riveter.

- About 12,000 women worked at Willow Run. They received the same pay as the men: from $.95 to $1.60 an hour.

- Workers built the last bomber, named Henry Ford, on June 24, 1945. But before it left the plant, Henry Ford requested that his name be removed from the nose of the ship and he had his employees sign their names instead.

- In 1947 the federal government sold Willow Run to the University of Michigan for $1.

- In 1977 the University of Michigan sold Willow Run to Wayne County for $1.

- Today Willow Run is one the biggest cargo airports in the country.

Making a Big Noise

Begun as a businessman's club in 1914, Kiwanis quickly moved beyond Michigan and evolved into a worldwide service organization of almost 300,000 members.

The early 20th century saw the birth of such clubs as Rotary International and the Exchange Club, in which businessmen could enjoy fellowship and engage in mutually beneficial transactions, often over a meal. In 1914 Allen Browne, a professional organizer, and Joseph Prance, a Detroit tailor, decided to develop a local fraternal club.

What's in a Name?

The club was first called the Supreme Lodge Benevolent Order Brothers, but the DOD acronym did not sit well with the members. When choosing a new name for the club, they chose to celebrate the Native American heritage of the Detroit area with the Otchipew phrase "Nun-Kee-wan-is," which was soon shortened to Kiwanis. The name has been alternately translated as "we trade," "we have a good time," and "we make a big noise." No matter how you translated it, the message was clear; the Kiwanis wanted to make its presence known.

A Change of Focus

The Kiwanis Club received its official charter on January 21, 1915, and grew quickly, but club members began to question Browne's role in the organization. Officially, he owned the Kiwanis name and received all membership dues. After an emotionally charged meeting in the summer of 1915, Browne left to start a club in Cleveland, and the Detroit Kiwanis Club rededicated itself to community service.

As the Kiwanis organization grew to nearly 100 clubs, the discontent with Browne's position as "owner" spread beyond Detroit, and the success of Kiwanis was actually Browne's undoing. The collective membership eventually grew tired of knowing that their community service organization was being used to turn a profit. Delegates to the 1919 International Convention offered to buy out Browne's interest in Kiwanis. Browne agreed to the sale, if the Kiwanians could raise $17,500 in 24 hours. They raised the amount in an hour, and Kiwanis became an independent organization.

In 1920 they officially adopted "We Build" as the Kiwanis motto, which reflected how the club had grown from a fellowship organization to one that also provided community service.

Kiwanis Today

The first club is still in existence, proudly calling itself Detroit Kiwanis Club #1, and over 8,000 other clubs have joined the Kiwanis ranks, with a membership totaling nearly 300,000. Kiwanis became an international organization soon after its creation with the chartering of the Hamilton, Ontario, Canada, club in 1916. There are currently Kiwanis clubs in 94 nations, on every continent except Antarctica.

Over the years, Kiwanis gave birth to several organizations that built upon its tradition of service: K-Kids for elementary school children, Builders Club at the middle school level, Key Club for high school students, Circle K for college students, Kiwanis Junior clubs for young adults in Europe, and Aktion clubs for people with disabilities. All told, Kiwanis and its sponsored programs have raised billions of dollars, performed countless hours of service, and changed lives around the globe. And it can all be traced back to a single group of community-minded Detroit businessmen.

KIWANIS BY THE NUMBERS

9.5 Average number of years a Kiwanis has been a member

14 Percent of Kiwanis members with masters' degrees

34 Percent of Kiwanis members employed in Banking/Finance—the largest employment field among its members.

38 Percent of Kiwanis members with bachelors' degrees

57 Average age of a Kiwanis member

502 Number of members in Kiwanis's largest club, in Birmingham, Alabama (as of June 2002)

1987 The year membership opened to women

299,005 Total membership in 2005

The Cherry Capital of the World

Every year Michigan's cherry production is about 250 million pounds, which represents about 75 percent of the tart cherries and 20 percent of the sweet cherries grown annually in the United States. Here's why Michigan's got cherries.

The sandy soil and temperate weather conditions along the eastern shore of Lake Michigan are excellent for growing fruit. That's because Lake Michigan was formed during the last Ice Age, some 12,000 years ago, by retreating glaciers that dug deep trenches in sandy areas that were once a seabed. Much of that sandy soil remains along the eastern shoreline. The winds blowing from Lake Michigan help to moderate the area's weather by cooling the orchards in the summer and warming them during the winter.

Some Cherry History

A Presbyterian missionary named Peter Dougherty first had the idea to plant cherry trees in the Traverse City area in 1852. Everyone told him cherries wouldn't grow that far north, but Dougherty's trees flourished. It didn't take long for other area residents to plant their own cherry trees.

Farmers soon began selling their cherries, which quickly created a market that seemed insatiable. As the demand increased, the farmers responded by planting more cherry trees. After Traverse City was linked by rail to Chicago and the rest of the country in 1872, more people moved to the area and took up cherry farming. By the 1880s large amounts of cherries were being shipped by boat to Chicago and Milwaukee. As the lumber industry stripped the hills surrounding Traverse City, farmers moved in and replanted the hills with cherry orchards. In 1893 Ridgewood Farm, the area's first commercial cherry orchard, was planted near the site of Dougherty's original orchard. Others followed. By the turn of the 20th century cherries had become the area's most important crop. Tons of cherries were being shipped all over the country via refrigerated train cars. The first cherry-processing facility, Traverse City Canning Company, was built just south of Traverse City.

National Cherry Festival

In 1925 the first cherry festival—the "Blessing of the Blossoms"—was held in Traverse City to generate publicity and expand the cherry market. It worked like a charm, and as demand continued to increase, many more orchards were planted along the eastern shore of Lake Michigan. The festival is now known as the National Cherry Festival and has grown into an eight-day celebration in July that attracts half a million visitors to Traverse City.

Today Traverse City is still the center of five key cherry-growing counties—Antrim, Benzie, Kalkaska, Leelanau, and

Grand Traverse—and about 3.8 million tart cherry trees and half a million sweet cherry trees grow in Michigan.

Sweet or Tart?

Sweet cherries are grown primarily for fresh eating, and the sweet cherry varieties grown in Michigan include Emperor Francis, Napoleon, and Schmidt. Maraschino cherries, used most often to top off ice cream sundaes or to dress up a cocktail, are made from sweet cherries.

The process for making maraschino cherries isn't very appetizing, but the end result is quite tasty. Sweet cherries are bleached in a brine solution of one percent sulfur dioxide and one-half percent unslaked lime for four to six weeks to remove most of the color. After that, they are pitted and bleached again with sodium chlorite. Then they are soaked in fresh water for a couple of days before sugar, red dyes, and an almond flavoring are added.

Tart cherries have a sour taste when eaten fresh, but they are excellent for baking. Montmorency is the most common variety of tart cherry used in jams, juices, preserves, and pie fillings. Tart cherries are extremely perishable, so they are harvested quickly and canned or frozen immediately.

The Health Benefits of Cherries

Since ancient times, cherry pits have been used to relieve a number of ailments including chest pains, stomach and intestinal spasms, throat irritation, and even labor pains.

Laboratory analysis reveals that cherries are rich in potassium, vitamin C, and B complex and they also contain antioxidants, melatonin, anthocyanins, and flavonoids. The health benefits of eating cherries include pain relief, the prevention of heart disease and cancer, the reduction of inflammation, and the lowering of uric acid.

The Cherry Pit Spit

In 1974 Herb Teichman, an Eau Claire, Michigan, cherry farmer, was looking for something to do and decided to organize a cherry-spitting competition with a few of his friends. The event quickly grew from a neighborhood get-together to an international competition, recognized by the *Guinness Book of World Records*.

Each July hundreds of people from around the world gather in Eau Claire for the competition. Among other practical considerations, the official rules stipulate that "denture racks will be provided for those who wish to remove their teeth."

Rick "Pellet Gun" Krause of Arizona has won the International Cherry Pit Spitting Championship 12 times since 1980. He held the world record with a distance of 72 feet, 7 inches until 1990, when his son Brian "Young Gun" Krause spit a cherry pit 72 feet, 11 inches. In 2003 Brian set another world record by launching a pit that flew an incredible 93 feet, 6 inches.

Cherry Facts

- An average tart cherry tree produces about 7,000 cherries. It takes about 250 tart cherries to make a cherry pie, so the average tree produces enough cherries for 28 pies.

- The average American consumes about one pound of tart cherries per year.

- The third week of July is usually the peak of the cherry harvest. Most sweet cherries are still picked by hand, but most tarts are harvested using a mechanical shaker.

- Cherry processors have efficient machines that remove cherry pits with minimal damage to the cherries and they even use pit detectors to eliminate any stray pits.

- The record for picking the most cherries by hand in one day was set in 1958 by 17-year-old Harold Robertson, who picked 1,225 pounds of cherries in one 12-hour period.

1926 CHERRY FESTIVAL

Beginning in 1926 the Cherry Festival Queen was selected by popular vote. Photos of the nominees were printed in the local paper along with a ballot. Charlotte Kearns won a decisive victory over the other candidates with 702 votes out of the more than 5,000. The same year, the tradition of baking a huge cherry pie and presenting it to the U.S. President began. The pie weighed 42 pounds, was three feet in diameter, and contained more than 5,000 cherries. It was loaded into a car via its tilting windshield and then placed in a wooden box in the back seat. It took three days to transport the pie to President Coolidge's summer home at White Pine Camp in upstate New York, but the pie arrived none the worse for wear.

Hometown: River View

Located outside of Flint, this bedroom community is known for its stellar view of the Flint River.

Town: Flushing
Location: Genesee County
Founding: 1877
Current population: 8,300 (est.)
Size: 4.3 square miles

What's in a Name?

Flushing was named in the 1830s after being founded by settlers from upstate New York and New England. The name is credited to Charles Seymour, who—along with his brother James—purchased the town in 1835 as a place to process harvested lumber. Charles had previously lived in Flushing, New York, and he gave his new Michigan town the same name after the state legislature rejected the proposed moniker of Dover. (Charles' New York relatives had roots in Vlissingen, Holland, which translates to "Flushing.")

Claim to Fame:

- Flushing is home to the Coffee Beanery national coffee chain, and it is also the headquarters for Eastman Outdoors, a leading manufacturer of outdoor cooking gear.

- The town is the setting for *The Situation in Flushing,* Edmund G. Love's autobiographical novel about growing up in small-town Michigan at the turn of the century.

- One of Flushing's native sons, Tom Luce, won a "Wheel of Fortune" championship in 1991. Luce took home $25,000 in cash and an Oriental rug estimated to be worth $7,000. (He also won a Corvette, but had to sell it because he could not afford the taxes on his then $6.25 per hour salary.)

- The town's old railroad depot burned down in the early 1980s, and its remains were donated to the Flushing Area Historical Society, which restored the site over a period of 13 years. The depot was rebuilt into what is now the Flushing Area Museum & Cultural Center.

- The Flushing Concert Band was conceived in 1849, and the Flushing Ladies Band from that general era was a precursor to the city's current "Concert in the Parks" series.

- The Flushing High Raider Marching Band has produced award-winning musicians. Flushing's Chamber of Commerce notes that "wherever they travel, their honors truly reflect the pride and tradition of excellence which reflect the Flushing spirit and history."

The Ten Cents Store

Attention, Kmart shoppers: the discount store you know today started with a single location on Detroit's Woodward Avenue. Founder Sebastian Spering Kresge created one of the retail industry's most successful chains and a charitable foundation that thrives long after his death.

Sebastian Kresge Jr. was born July 31, 1867, in Bald Mount, Pennsylvania, to farmers Sebastian and Catherine Kresge. Sebastian decided early that he was ill suited to the family business, noting it depended too much on the weather. So he struck a deal with his parents. He would turn over all of his wages until he was 21 if they covered his college tuition. They agreed and during those years, the young Kresge raised bees, delivered groceries, sold insurance, and even ran a bakery.

During a stint as a bookkeeper at a local hardware store, Kresge noticed some rusty stoves in a back corner. "On his own time, he repaired, cleaned, and polished the stoves—and, to everyone's surprise, sold them, proving he was an amazingly good salesman," Stanley Kresge wrote in a memoir of his father. "The stoves started him on the road to success." That road led to Bertels Sons and Co., a specialty hardware store where Kresge became a salesman. During his travels, Kresge called on Frank Winfield Woolworth, who had started a five-and-dime store. He studied Woolworth's approach, impressed that his business had survived the Depression.

A lifetime teetotaler, Kresge lived modestly, rarely eating in restaurants. The Depression of 1893 cemented his frugal nature. In five years Kresge had saved an impressive $8,000. He approached Woolworth as an investor but was turned down. He turned to another customer, J.G. McCrory. They became partners, opening their first five-and-dime stores in Memphis and Detroit. Kresge wanted to expand, but McCrory did not, so the two partners split in 1899. Kresge kept the Detroit store, located on busy Woodward Avenue.

Shopping for Peanuts

Recalling his childhood, Kresge knew how hard it was for working-class families. He felt everyone should be able to buy products at prices they could afford. So he made the shop's motto, "Nothing over ten cents in store." By 1912 he had 85 stores and annual profits of $10 million. The S.S. Kresge Company became a publicly traded company on the New York Stock Exchange in 1918. "I think I was successful because I was willing to work, because I saved, and because I heeded good advice," Kresge told the Associated Press.

After World War II, Kresge's company developed a new store model—to purchase merchandise in high volume so everything could be sold at lower prices. This became the model used in the Kmart stores. The first Kmart opened in Garden City in 1962 and was a huge success. The company opened 17 more stores that year, leading to profits of over $450 million.

How to Become a Billionaire Philanthropist

Kresge was notoriously cheap. He once told *The Detroit News* that he "never spent more than 30 cents for lunch in my life." His first two of three wives divorced him, complaining of his thrifty nature. Still, Kresge possessed a generosity of spirit. He established the Kresge Foundation in 1925, the year he retired, to celebrate his company's silver anniversary. Its goal was to "promote the well-being of mankind," Kresge said. He donated over $60 million to the Foundation over the next 42 years. Its main purpose is to provide grants to schools, scientists, and businesses. To this day, the Foundation follows his basic tenants—it does not invest in companies that make the majority of their profits from alcohol or tobacco.

Kresge's best-known quote came in 1953 at the dedication of Kresge Hall at Harvard University's Business School. Asked to speak, Kresge rose and said, "I never made a dime talking." Then he sat back down.

Kresge continued to serve as chairman of the company until 1966. He died October 18 of that year from complications from pneumonia. The stores honored him by closing for one hour. At that time, 172 Kmart stores and 753 Kresge locations had sales topping the $1 billion mark.

In 1976 the company changed its name to Kmart Corporation to represent the new store format's domination. In 1987 Kmart sold the remainder of its Kresge store holdings to his old partner's company, McCrory Stores. It changed its name to Kmart Holding Corporation after surviving a 2002 bankruptcy. All that remains of Kresge's legacy at Kmart is his initial, emblazoned on the stores' signs nationwide.

The World's First Muscle Car

Ever seen—or heard—a muscle car? They were big sellers in the mid-1960s, but by the early 1970s they were gone. From Slightly Irregular, *here's a look at the car that started it all: the Pontiac GTO.*

Breakdown

In the summer of 1956 General Motors appointed an engineer named Semon "Bunkie" Knudsen general manager of the company's Pontiac division. Knudsen's marching orders were simple: he had five years to improve the division's sales and if he couldn't do it, GM might shut Pontiac down for good.

In those days Pontiac was America's sixth largest automaker. The cars were affordable and reliable, but they were slow and their styling was outdated; they were the kind of cars that grandparents drove. That was the biggest problem, Knudsen figured. "You can sell a young man's car to an old man," he liked to say, "but you'll never sell an old man's car to a young man." Knudsen hired E.M. "Pete" Estes, formerly the chief engineer at Oldsmobile, to head the engineering department, and he hired a 31-year-old Packard engineer named John Z. DeLorean to be Estes's assistant. Changes came quickly: They immediately began manufacturing high-performance versions of their existing models. The following year they created the Pontiac Bonneville, a racy full-sized convertible with a big V-8 engine and fancy bucket seats.

Wide-Tracking

For 1959 Knudsen had the designers come up with a new wide-bodied car with extra-wide tires to boot. These "Wide-Track" Pontiacs had an athletic, broad-shouldered look that caught on quickly with younger drivers. By 1960 they were the best-selling midpriced car in the country. By 1961 Pontiac had done so well that Knudsen was promoted to general manager of Chevrolet. Pete Estes replaced him as the head of Pontiac, and John DeLorean became the chief engineer. Together, they were about to come up with the most famous Pontiac ever.

Out of the Race

From 1959 to 1963, Pontiac had dominated the NASCAR circuit with their custom-built race cars, but then GM decided to stop producing them so they could focus on selling higher-profit consumer vehicles. Employees in all auto divisions were banned from any participation in motorsports. They weren't even allowed to assist professional race car drivers. Estes was miffed about the restriction—he didn't want to lose the association with sports. So he decided that if he couldn't put a race car on a racetrack, he'd start putting them on the street. He and DeLorean used the same trick that hot-rodders had used for years: They took the giant engine out of the full-sized Pontiac Bonneville and dropped it into the midsized Pontiac Tempest/LeMans. They added lots of other goodies, too: high performance carburetors, a heavy-duty clutch and suspension, dual chrome exhausts, an air scoop on the front hood, and an optional four-speed manual transmission with a stick shift on the floor.

Secret Weapon

It's not uncommon for auto companies to hide new models from the public, but Estes and DeLorean hid it from their bosses at GM. Putting such a huge engine into a car that small was against company rules, so rather than introduce the car as a new model, they called it an "option package" for the Pontiac LeMans, hoping that nobody would realize what they were up to.

DeLorean named the souped up LeMans the GTO, which was short for Gran Turisimo Omologato. *Omologato* is the Italian word for homologous, which means "all coming from the same thing." Whereas most custom-built hot rods of the time were pieced together from different cars and "aftermarket" parts, the GTO was truly homologous—all of its parts came from Pontiac. This made it America's first "factory hot rod," or "muscle car." Calling the GTO an option package for the LeMans paid off: by the time the bosses at GM realized what was happening, car dealers had already placed orders for 5,000 of the cars, so GM grudgingly agreed to let the car be built. Whatever anger the company bosses had toward Estes and DeLorean disappeared when more than 32,000 GTOs sold that first model year alone, and 75,000 in 1965.

The car was a smash hit, and GM not only allowed the GTO to become a model in its own right for 1966 (it sold nearly 97,000 cars that year), it also made plans for its other divisions to produce their own muscle cars, including the

Chevy Chevelle SS, the Buick Regal Gran Sport, and the
Oldsmobile Cutlass 442.

Muscle Cars Everywhere

Over the next few years the other Big Three automakers got
into the act too: Ford introduced the Fairlane GT, the Mercury
Cyclone GT, and the Ford Torino Cobra. Chrysler came out
with the Dodge Charger and the Plymouth Road Runner, to
name just a few. Each year the engines got bigger and more
powerful. The 1964 Pontiac GTO had a 325 horsepower
engine; by 1971 the Plymouth Road Runner had a 425 horsepower engine.

End of the Road

Muscle cars were popular because they were cheap and fast—a
brand-new 1964 GTO convertible cost only $3,081—and
though many got less than ten miles to the gallon, gas only
cost about 25 cents a gallon so it wasn't a problem. Tens of
thousands took muscle cars to the road in the late 1960s and
early 1970s. And then by 1973 they were gone.

What happened? For one thing, when the auto insurance
industry realized that muscle cars were little more than street-
legal race cars, they raised their rates so high that many people
paid more for insurance than they did for their monthly car
payment. Then in 1973 the Arab oil embargo caused the price
of gasoline to soar. Suddenly cheap muscle cars weren't so
cheap anymore. To make things worse, they were also coming
under increased criticism from environmentalists and car-safety
advocates.

The automakers were also being pressured by the federal government to build more fuel-efficient cars that could run on regular or unleaded gas. In 1974 Pontiac came out with a muscle car without any muscle, a GTO with only 200 horsepower. In 1975 they didn't even bother. The GTO bit the dust, just like nearly every other muscle car it inspired.

If you missed your chance to own a GTO, cheer up. Pontiac brought a new one to market in 2004. Price: $32,495, quite a lot more than a new GTO cost forty years ago, but about as much as you can expect a classic GTO in excellent condition to cost you today.

CAPTAIN KID

In April 2003 the community of Houghton became the scene for one of the most high-profile pirate capers of the 21st century. Joe Nievelt, a student at Michigan Technological University, was sued for piracy: music piracy. The Recording Industry Association of America (RIAA; a United States music industry watchdog group) sued Joe and three other cyber swashbucklers for setting up illegal computer systems to distribute copyrighted music files. The damages sought by the RIAA? A hefty $150,000 . . . per song. In Nievelt's case, that added up to about $97.8 billion (more than the entire music industry even makes in a year). Thankfully, Joe didn't have to face the gallows: the case was settled out of court for about $15,000.

Pistons by the Numbers

The Detroit Pistons franchise is among the oldest in professional basketball, starting out as the Fort Wayne (Indiana) Pistons in 1941 and moving to Detroit in 1957. But Detroit hoops fans didn't have much to cheer about until Isiah Thomas and the team known as "The Bad Boys" arrived in the 1980s.

0 Number of Pistons team members who have won the league's Most Valuable Player award

1 Piston officials who have been named the National Basketball Assocation's Executive of the Year (Joe Dumars, 2003)

2 Piston coaches who have been named NBA Coach of the Year (Ray Scott, 1974; Rick Carlisle, 2002)

3 Pistons who have won the league's Rookie of the Year Award (Don Meineke, 1953; Dave Bing, 1967; Grant Hill, 1995)

7 Numbers retired by the Pistons (2, Chuck Daly; 4, Joe Dumars; 11, Isiah Thomas; 15, Vinnie Johnson; 16, Bob Lanier; 21, Dave Bing; 40, Bill Lambier)

9 Pistons in the Basketball Hall of Fame (Dave Bing, Harry Gallatin, Bob Lanier, George Yardley, Alex English, Bailey Howell, Bob McAdoo, Isiah Thomas, and Larry Brown)

13 Consecutive seasons the Pistons posted losing records after moving to Detroit in 1957. It wasn't until the 1970–71 season that Detroit fans had a winning team.

24 Dave DeBusschere's age in 1964 when he was named player-coach of the Pistons. He is the youngest head coach ever in the National Basketball Association. DeBusschere coached the team until late in the 1966–67 season.

27.8 George Yardley's average in the 1957–58 season, the Pistons's first season in Detroit, when he led the league in points per game

.195 Winning percentage for the 1979–80 Pistons (16–66), which was also the worst record in the league

.768 Winning percentage for the 1988–89 Pistons (63–19), which was the best record in the league

$35 million Purchase price for the Pistons in 1974, when the team was bought by a consortium led by Detroit businessman William Davidson. In 2004 the franchise was valued at an estimated $284 million.

THE BAD BOYS

In 1981, using the second overall pick in the NBA draft, Detroit selected Isiah Thomas, a guard from Indiana University. Thomas, along with future teammates Vinnie Johnson, Bill Lambier, Joe Dumars, Rick Mahorn, Dennis Rodman, and others, led a resurgence of the team culminating in back-to-back World Championships in 1989 and 1990.

Walk the Plank? No, Drive It

*You think the roads are bad now? Be thankful
you're not living back in the mid-1800s.
Things were worse then. Much worse.*

Early Beginnings

In the early to mid-1800s, many Americans headed westward,
packing their possessions and families onto wagons and stage-
coaches that rolled along the bumpy dirt paths, which quickly
turned to mud when it rained. Finally someone had the bright
idea to lay down wooden planks in the road to straddle the
uneven dirt and mud. These new "plank roads" could cut a trip
from five days down to twelve hours.

And whom can we thank for this traffic time-saver?
Michiganders, of course. In 1837 Michigan legislation
approved the Detroit, Plymouth, and Ann Arbor turnpike company to lay plank roads along the most popular paths. New
York likes to claim they were first with the idea, but Michigan
had them beat by about five years.

The Road Takes Its Toll

Of course, nothing is free. Early on, Michigan didn't have a highway advisory committee, so privately run companies created the plank roads, which cost from $1,000 to $3,000 per mile. When laying a plank road, builders included a small wooden structure about the size and shape of an outhouse to be erected every five miles. Thus, the creation of the tollbooth. If you wanted to travel the road, you would have to pay the following:

Two-horse-drawn carriage: 2 cents per mile

More than two horses: additional 3/4 cent per mile

One-horse-drawn carriage: 1 cent per mile

A score of sheep: 1/2 cent per mile (were the owners fleeced by the tolls?)

A score of cattle: 2 cents per mile

Over time, clever travelers found a way around paying the tolls—exiting the road before the tollgate then reentering further down.

A Bumpy Ride

While the plank roads did save time, they weren't the most comfortable. The population of Michigan more than tripled in the years between 1840 and 1860, which meant many more horse-drawn carriages roughing up those wooden roads—which were never intended to handle such traffic. To make matters even worse, the planks decayed and warped over time, causing unsteady footholds for the horses. Because lumber costs were high, sometimes gravel was used to fill holes. The combination did not make for a smooth ride. When Mark

Twain was asked how he enjoyed his ride on a plank road from Kalamazoo, he quipped "It would have been good if some unconscionable scoundrel had not now and then dropped a plank across it."

End of the Road

Plank roads had run their course by 1900, but they paved the way for a settled Michigan. Detroit was the center hub from which eight plank roads radiated out. Some of those roads today are East and West Jefferson avenues and Grand River, Woodward, Gratiot, and Michigan avenues. The plank roads were replaced by gravel—and none too soon, as Henry Ford was soon to revolutionize the automobile industry with the establishment of his Ford Motor Company in 1903. And eventually railroad lines replaced many plank roads.

So when you bemoan your daily commute, just remember to thank those early Michiganders for getting the ball rolling—without them, it could take you a lot longer to get home.

THEN AND NOW

In 1850 the Detroit & Howell Plank Road coupled with the Howell & Lansing Plank Road and later evolved into today's U.S. 16. In 1995 road crews were reconstructing Grand River Avenue in East Lansing when they found a series of logs lying two feet below the road surface. The logs were quickly identified as the remnants of the Lansing & Howell Plank Road.

Treasures from the Deep

Thousands of ships have sunk in Lake Michigan over the years. And where there are sunken ships there might be sunken treasure.

- **Black Hawk** Rumored to have sunk in 1862 during the Civil War near Point Betsie, Michigan, with a cargo including gold bullion.

- **Java** Said to have sunk in 1878 in 200 feet of water near Big Sable Point, taking its coins and bullion to the lake's bottom.

- **Venus** Lost in 1887 near Thunder Bay, it is said to have been carrying a government payroll in gold and silver coins.

- **Pere Marquette** Sank near Ludington in 1910 reportedly with gold and silver coins and more than two dozen loaded railroad cars.

However, the Holy Grail of sunken treasures is five chests of gold, lost somewhere between Michigan and Wisconsin.

The Legend Goes...

In 1862 or 1863 an unnamed Canadian vessel sailed from Michigan with five chests of gold worth about $20 million. The money came from England and was bound for the United

States Confederacy. As with all treasure stories, there are conflicting versions. The ship was intercepted and to avoid losing the gold, the crew tied the chests together and threw them overboard. That $20 million in gold coins from the 1860s translates into about $300 to $400 million in today's currency. Not surprisingly, the search for this gold has been fierce. But the search isn't for the faint of heart. The water in this area is very cold (40° F), 20 to 70 feet deep, and the lake's bottom is extremely rocky.

Richard Bennett has launched numerous expeditions to track down the vessel and its treasure. When he was younger, Bennett worked with Mel Fisher on the *Nuestra Senora* salvage operation. He has put this experience to work on the Lake Michigan project in the form of both scuba diving expeditions and submarine construction.

Another contender who has embraced the challenge is Steven Libert, who says he has spent more than 35 years and $25,000 researching the treasure. He launched a federal court battle with a high-powered attorney to claim ownership of a recent find near Poverty Island. Maritime legal experts say this type of motion is common prior to launching a salvage operation, because Michigan typically tries to claim ownership of historic shipwrecks under the Abandoned Shipwreck Act.

It's still uncertain whether Libert has discovered the lost gold, or simply one of the many ships that lies at the bottom of Lake Michigan. In any case, he may have indeed found a historical treasure. The French government believes the ship is the 17th century barque *Le Griffen,* and they are filing their own claim.

Answers

What's So Great About the Great Lakes? page 13

1. Ontario
2. Michigan
3. Superior
4. Erie
5. Chicago; Michigan
6. Superior; Isle Royale is a roadless, wilderness archipelago that is accessible only by boat or float plane.
7. Michigan
8. Superior
9. Huron and Michigan; the Mackinac Bridge joins the upper and lower peninsulas of Michigan.
10. Michigan, Huron, and Erie

I Want My M(ichigan) TV!, page 39

1. B

2. B

3. C

4. A

5. C

6. A

Celebrity Michigan, page 52

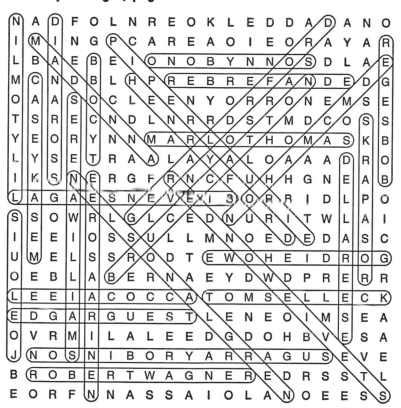

A Model Puzzle, page 88

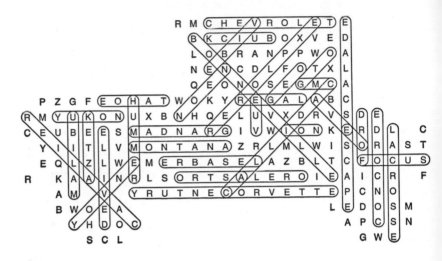

Do You Speak Michigan? page 157

1. B. Big Beaver Exit

2. B. Yous guys or youse guys

3. B. Porkie. For more on pasties, see page 54. Cudighi is a ground pork dish popular in the Upper Peninsula. It's often used as the meat in Italian dishes and sometimes used in pork link sausages.

4. A. The Upper Peninsula

5. A trick question, as the correct answer is both A and C

6. B. AA doesn't fly with Ann Arborites.

7. C. The Gulf of Winnebago

8. A. The Porcupine Mountains

9. C. The center of the Lower Peninsula. If you look closely
    at the state of Michigan, you'll notice that it's shaped like a
    mitten. St. Louis, Michigan, is the geographic center of the
    Lower Peninsula or the "middle of the mitten." The book
    Saint Louis, Michigan: The Middle-of-the-Mitten City by
    Ellen Perry documents the expression.

10. B. A popular and peculiarly Michigan card game, played
    with four people (two teams), and similar to Spades and
    Bridge in that the object of the game is to take tricks

11. A. The Michigan library card, which was phased in to
    include all Michigan libraries in 2000

12. A. The Fab 5 were Chris Webber, Jimmy King, Jalen Rose,
    Juwan Howard, and Ray Jackson.

Scoring

11–12: You are probably a native of Michigan.

9–10: You have lived in Michigan for a significant part of your
life.

7–8: You probably live in Canada and do a reverse commute to
Michigan to work.

5–6: You were an out-of-state student who flunked out of a
Michigan university or college.

3–4: You had better get a Michicard and use it often.

2 and below: You grew up in Ohio and will be arrested immediately upon setting foot on Michigan soil.

Road Shows, page 166

E	L	H	I	■	C	O	M	M	A	■	A	R	C	O
R	O	O	M	■	O	N	E	U	P	■	L	E	A	N
E	T	N	A	■	I	T	A	L	O	■	I	C	U	S
C	H	O	C	O	L	A	T	E	C	H	E	E	S	E
T	A	L	■	T	S	P	S	■	■	E	N	D	A	T
E	R	U	P	T	■	■	A	L	L	■	E	L	S	■
R	I	L	E	■	G	Y	M	B	A	G	S	■	■	■
■	O	U	T	H	O	U	S	E	R	A	C	E	S	■
■	■	A	R	A	L	S	E	A	■	O	Y	E	R	■
H	R	H	■	O	D	E	■	■	O	P	E	R	A	■
A	E	O	N	S	■	■	D	A	M	A	■	L	E	S
D	I	N	O	S	A	U	R	G	A	R	D	E	N	S
A	S	I	F	■	S	L	O	A	N	■	O	V	A	L
G	E	N	L	■	C	N	O	T	E	■	M	E	D	E
O	R	G	Y	■	H	A	L	E	S	■	O	L	E	S

Bragging Rights, page 182

L	A	S	T	■	F	E	E	S	■	B	E	B	O	P
U	C	L	A	■	A	X	L	E	■	A	L	A	M	O
L	O	O	T	■	S	T	A	R	■	L	I	R	A	S
L	I	M	E	S	T	O	N	E	Q	U	A	R	R	Y
S	N	O	R	K	E	L	■	■	U	S	N	■	■	■
■	■	■	T	I	N	■	M	E	A	T	■	O	B	I
E	R	G	O	■	E	P	I	C	■	E	F	L	A	T
R	E	D	T	A	R	T	C	H	E	R	R	I	E	S
S	P	A	S	M	■	A	R	O	N	■	A	E	R	O
T	O	Y	■	A	L	S	O	■	D	O	C	■	■	■
■	■	■	I	T	E	■	■	E	G	O	T	R	I	P
P	O	T	T	E	D	G	E	R	A	N	I	U	M	S
E	L	I	H	U	■	E	X	A	M	■	O	N	E	A
S	E	D	E	R	■	R	I	S	E	■	N	E	A	T
O	G	E	E	S	■	E	T	E	S	■	S	S	N	S

Official Business, page 195

1. D	6. B
2. B	7. C
3. D	8. A
4. C	9. C
5. D	10. A

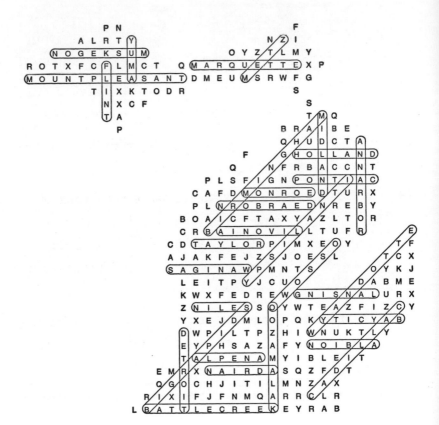

Which Michigander Am I? page 228

1. Pam Dawber. The TV programs she was in were "Mork & Mindy" (with Robin Williams) and "My Sister Sam" (with Rebecca Schaeffer). She's married to actor Mark Harmon.

2. Robert Jarvik. His first artificial heart was the Jarvik 7. His current thumb-sized pump is known as the Jarvik 2000.

3. Derek Jeter. He currently plays shortstop with the New York Yankees.

4. James Earl Jones. His most famous role is as the voice of Darth Vader (who was played physically by David Prowse in the first three films, and by Hayden Christensen in *Star Wars Episode III: The Revenge of the Sith*). His first film role was in Kubrick's *Dr. Strangelove*.

5. Windsor McKay. His famous comic strip was "Little Nemo in Slumberland"; the dinosaur cartoon was called "Gertie the Dinosaur."

6. Larry Page. He and Sergey Brin created the Google Internet search engine